S0-CDR-209

A Voice From Colorado's Past for the Present

HARRIS & EWING

A VOICE FROM COLORADO'S PAST FOR THE PRESENT

SELECTED WRITINGS OF GEORGE NORLIN

Selected and Edited by Ralph E. Ellsworth

COLORADO ASSOCIATED UNIVERSITY PRESS

Published by Colorado Associated University Press
Boulder, Colorado 80309
International Standard Book Number 0-87081-157-6
Library of Congress Catalog Card Number 85-72909
Printed in the United States of America

All royalties from the sale of this book will be donated to
the Norlin Library Book Fund at the University of Colorado

Colorado Associated University Press is a cooperative publishing enterprise supported in part by Adams State College, Colorado State University, Fort Lewis College, Mesa College, Metropolitan State College, University of Colorado, University of Northern Colorado, University of Southern Colorado, and Western State College

For
Agnes Norlin

CONTENTS

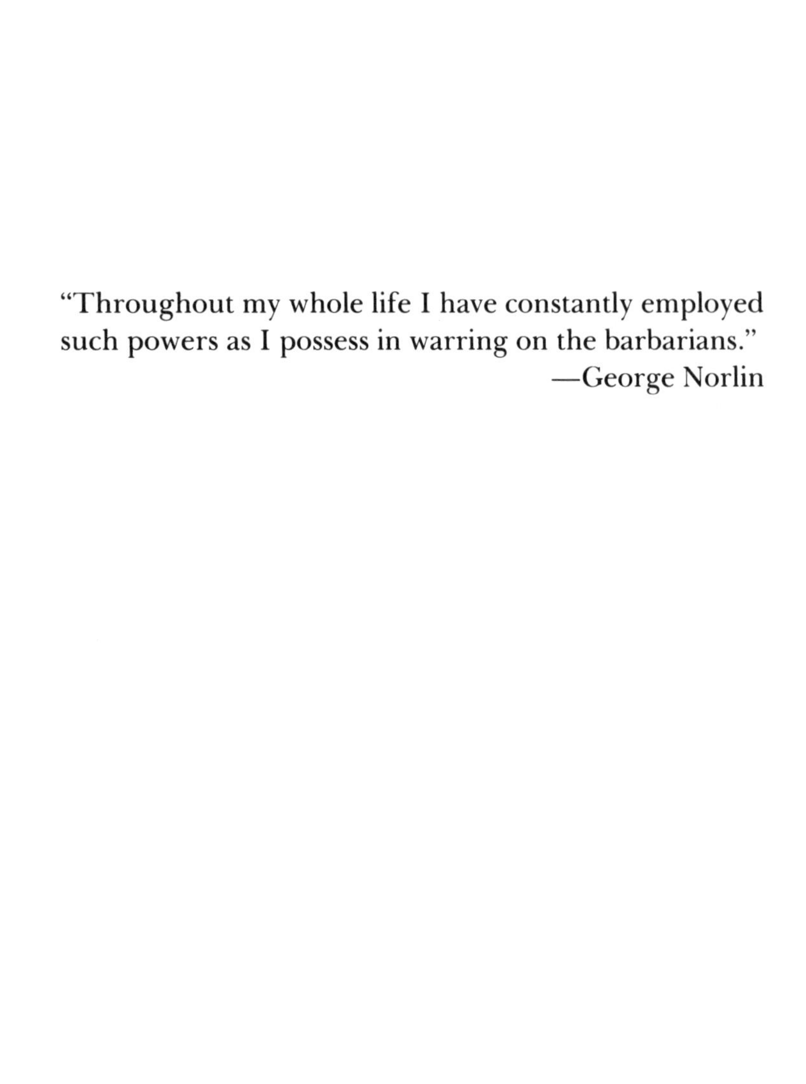

"Throughout my whole life I have constantly employed such powers as I possess in warring on the barbarians."

—George Norlin

INTRODUCTION

For six years prior to his death in 1942, George Norlin was my good friend and neighbor. For four of those six years he was my president at the University of Colorado. For one delightful month in 1940 at the Faculty Ranch it was my privilege to fish for trout, play poker, and spend whole days visiting with him. Elevated to the presidency of the university by the faculty, he was a genuinely modest man of many and unselfish gifts—a prolific author, an accomplished teacher, and a superlative administrator. The late literary critic Dixon Wecter called him "the first citizen of Colorado" and thought him "the only first-class scholar among university presidents in the West."

Norlin was born near Concordia, Kansas in 1871, the son of Swedish immigrants. He attended the public schools in Concordia and, later, in Fish Creek, Wisconsin. His brief employment as an overqualified clerk for the Rock Island Railroad in Kansas prompted him to consider alternatives, among them Hastings College in Nebraska. He enrolled the following September, graduated in 1893, and then taught Greek at the college for the next three years.

During the summer months between academic years, Norlin studied at the University of Chicago where he came under the spell of Paul Shorey, an international authority on Plato. Shorey invited him to apply for a fellowship in the graduate school. Norlin accepted, and from Shorey, Wecter wrote, Norlin "gained a sense of the unity of learning, of measuring the American Constitution by the yardstick of Aristotle of reading Aristophanes in the light of modern sociology." Three years later Norlin was awarded the Ph.D., *magna cum laude*.

During a summer holiday in Boulder, Colorado, Norlin's first sight of the snow-capped Rocky Mountains, the clear air and sunlight made it easy for him to accept an offer to teach classics at the University of Colorado. As he remembered the occasion, he was appointed to the faculty by a gruff but kindly president who, "when he wanted to pat you on the back he did it with his foot."

In the autumn of 1901, Norlin went abroad to study the manuscripts of Theocritis at the *Bibliothèque Nationale* in Paris. Then after a semester at the Sorbonne, he set out for Greece and Asia Minor to explore the site of ancient Troy. He spent the spring of his *wanderjahr* in Sicily, at Taormina, the land of Theocritis, returning in the fall to Colorado—and to teaching, "that fellowship of folly and hope," as he once described his chosen profession. When war broke out in Europe, Livingston Farrand, the president of the university, took a leave of absence to direct the activities of the American Red Cross. Norlin was asked to serve as the acting president—"an emergency measure," Norlin insisted. These were the days before the search committee had been invented, and when Farrand resigned in 1919, the faculty unanimously asked that Norlin be kept as their permanent president. He is reported to have accepted with "reluctance," then served the university with great distinction for twenty years.

Norlin retired in 1939. But even today, nearly half a century after his death, he continues to exert a benevolent influence over the university community through the lasting impressions he made on his faculty, the students, and his many friends. He was one of those rare persons that make a difference in our lives, for he had an abundance of those qualities we all admire: courage in the face of adversity, compassion for his fellow men, a sense of decency, tenacity, an earthy sense of humor, and great wisdom about the common things of everyday living. His professional ideals and his sound personal values, eloquently expressed in the essays and speeches that follow, are as relevant today as they were when he first wrote them, for after a decade of economic deprivation and consequent demoralization in the world of higher education, we badly need to hear again from one who so strongly believed in the enduring worth of the traditional goals of a university education.

Ralph E. Ellsworth
Director of Libraries and
Professor Emeritus

The University of Colorado, Boulder
June 1985

· I ·

EARLY YEARS

George Norlin seldom talked about his youth or his family, so I was pleasantly surprised when I discovered among his papers in the Western History Collections in Norlin Library at the University of Colorado in Boulder the following unpublished autobiographical account of his early years in Kansas and Wisconsin.

There is no date on this typescript, but since Norlin tells us he is writing "about a boyhood fifty years removed," it must have been written after he retired from the University of Colorado, perhaps 1939 or 1940.

A LIFE

1. The Old Country

In early June of 1933, while occupying the *Theodore Roosevelt Chair of American Life and Institutions* in the University of Berlin, I visited for the first time Sweden, the land of my fathers. It may seem strange that up to then I had felt no special urge to tread the soil which had nurtured my people for generations. I had been abroad some thirty years before as a student and seen much of Europe, but other countries then seemed more to my purpose and Sweden was remote from my thoughts.

But was it strange, really? My immediate family had come to America shortly before I was born. But by the time I was old enough to be awake to what was going on around me I was in a home which was by no means a bit of old Sweden. English had all but crowded out Swedish as the language of our household—a fact that I was to rue later when in Sweden I found that my knowledge of the mother tongue was so slight that I was obliged to converse with my blood relations there, to my great embarrassment, in whatever foreign language they had most at their command (German or French or English) rather than in the language of our common stock! In other respects, too, we were pretty well Americanized. My family had rooted themselves quickly in the new soil and were preoccupied largely with their adopted country. To give only one example, I recall clearly the gloom which fell upon our household when President Garfield was assassinated. No scions of Pilgrim stock could have shared more loyally in the nation's sorrow.

Not that the ties which bound my parents to their life across the water were sharply broken. I often heard them talk together of the old country (*gamla landet*) in fond reminiscence. Also, scattered about our house were family albums and photographs of Swedish scenes, which they manifestly cherished, and which I, when the weather kept me indoors and there was nothing more enticing to do, thumbed over with mild curiosity. But all that seemed far away and long ago and to have nothing to do with me.

Indeed I felt on the defensive because my family were immigrants and I myself had narrowly escaped being one. As I look back over three score years, that sentiment seems incredibly silly, yet easily explained. The boys in our neighborhood made me feel at times that my foreignness was a bar sinister, though I was in fact no more outlandish than most of them. When I crossed them in any way they would taunt me with being a "Swede"—an appellation which was neither intended as a compliment nor received as such. I might mention in passing a delightful case in point, when a Swedish boy in a quarrel with another of the same extraction called his compatriot a "Swede," the other retorting with equal venom, "Swede, yourself!" As for me, I was absurdly sensitive and resented such contumely as a *casus belli*, though I must confess that I battled with my little Scandinavian fists, not to vindicate the respectability of my provenance, of which I myself had no appreciation then, but to establish my due place amongst them.

This having to do battle was, I believe, a valuable propaedeutic; for, as Victor Hugo says somewhere, those who really live are those who battle, *Ceaux qui vivent ce sont ceaux qui luttent*; but its effect upon me then and for years to come was that I felt no attachment for the old country but wanted rather to be cut off from such associations.

However, in 1933 the circumstances were very different. Sweden, which had once held the attention of the world as an aggressive military power and then had fallen into the obscurity that is the lot of those who give themselves over to the arts of peace, had now again seized upon the popular imagination as an enviable country where one might fine refuge and repose from a nerve-wracked world (a near-fulfillment of the ancient legend of the Hyperboreans): and I was at an age when being "cut off" proves to be a loneliness—when the rank self-sufficiency of youth begins to fade into a wistfulness to find prop and comfort in some continuity of blood and race.

I once heard an Englishman say in justification of his adherence to the Established Church, though he was not a religious devotee, that he wanted to go to heaven or hell with his ancestors. I could understand something of his feeling, though not in like degree, having grown up in a land of refugees where a man's worth must be reckoned by what he is in himself and where ancestry is often forgotten and sometimes better forgotten. Yet, not knowing if ever again I might cross the Atlantic from my faraway home in the Rocky Mountains, I felt that I must no longer neglect the country of my ancestors.

Moreover, I was lecturing in Germany on liberalism in American history while the Hitler regime was expunging every vestige and prompting of liberalism from the German Reich. The atmosphere was stifling and I felt desperately the need of clean air. Sweden was not far away and the Whitsuntide vacation was at hand.

Never were holidays so welcome, and gladly my wife and I took advantage of this intermission to make our northern pilgrimage.

We set foot on Swedish soil with the eager unease one has on entering a strange country, but before we had rolled many hours on the early express from Malmo to Stockholm we began to feel at home. The coffee at breakfast was, for the first time in months, what coffee should be: a delectable adjutant of the quickening dawn. The nightmare of a crashing civilization lay behind us for a time. The air was sweet, the countryside restful. Here it seemed that the old warfare between nature and man had been composed in a lasting peace, the well-kept human habitations and farmsteads having been fitted into the charm of innumerable lakes and forests, leaving room for freedom. The words of Virgil, *O fortunatos nimium*, spoken enviously of those who lived simply and quietly on the Roman countryside, came to my lips as applicable to these people, who were not oppressed by crowding nor as yet fearful of nations warring for Lebensraum. We found them uniformly friendly and obliging as people in happy circumstances are wont to be. By the time we reached Stockholm, beautiful city of many waters, we were in love with Sweden and her people, and we felt, as I have said, at home.

Yet in one respect we found it hard to orient ourselves. Accustomed as we were to the principle of *caveat emptor*, we experienced something lacking and disconcerting in the Swedish character. I marked it on a visit to a tourist bureau on our first day in Stockholm. I had thought of Sweden as a little country which could be envisaged almost at a glance, but a whole day's journey by fast express from Malmo to the Capital—only one-fourth of the land's long reach from north to south—had disabused me of that ignorance, and I sought out the tourist bureau to be advised as to how best to see as much of it as our brief holiday permitted.

The manager was very courteous and sympathetic, but not, I thought, accommodating. He was disinclined to fit me out with tickets. "You should have at least a whole summer to see Sweden in," he said; "if your time is so limited you had better stay in Stockholm and make short trips from here."

What a salesman! I thought. Imagine a tourist agent in Paris or Naples or Los Angeles reluctant to sell to a customer eager to buy! I took his advice. I knew it was disinterested, yet I took it somewhat painfully and resentfully not only because I was disappointed in my expectations but that I was disturbed by this "transvaluation of all values." Habits, good or bad, are not painlessly upset.

Nor was that an exceptional experience. There was no high-pressure salesmanship in evidence anywhere—no commercial allurements and enchantments, no hypnotizing of the customer into buying what in his right mind he does not want nor feel the need of. On the contrary, there was a consideration for the tourist which could easily be interpreted as indifference and was, indeed, a bit discomfiting at first. The Swedes, I said to myself, are a simple, guileless people, but they don't fit into the modern scheme of things. Their virtue is their vice; they lack the supreme quality of acquisitiveness; they are poor business men.

I was not, however, taken entirely by surprise. I have noted this same characteristic in the Scandinavian settlers in this country. I well remember from my boyhood on our Kansas farm an incident which seems amusing now though it frightened me at the time. A neighbor, himself an immigrant from Sweden, had been hauling manure to fertilize our garden. The hauling done, he drove up to the house and presented his bill. My father was much displeased because he had charged too little—his work was worth much more than that. The other with equal displeasure insisted that he knew what was right and would take not a cent more. Here were two irresistible stubbornnesses in head-on collision. There was a crash of violent language, which was about to end in blows when my mother, the great pacificator of our neighborhood, appeared on the scene and poured oil upon the quarrel. Which of the belligerents gave way, I do not remember. I can only say that I never knew my father to yield an inch from what he thought was just and right, least of all when his sense of justice worked to his own damage.

2. *My Family Migrates to the New World*

I have spoken of that episode as amusing, but I wonder whether "amusing" is just the right world. I leave that interesting question unanswered. The answer is not pertinent here. What is pertinent is the fact that this idiosyncrasy gave direction to my life. To speak more definitely, I owe my birth on American soil to the fact that my father, being a Swede, was a poor business man. He was not a shrewd man; on the contrary, he was all but naive in his trustfulness. He had been easily persuaded to back with his signature a grandiose enterprise which went to smash and left him holding the sack at a time when a series of crop failures had already put his back to the wall. He was unable to meet his obligations, and his very considerable landed estate was put upon the auction block and sold at a great sacrifice. He managed to save something out of the wreck, but far too little to enable a family of eleven (there were nine children) to hold up their heads in the social milieu to which they belonged; and to lose caste in the Sweden of those days was insufferable.

What then, to do? My father could have reentered the Swedish army in which he had been an officer. But the pay of a military career was more in social distinction than in money. Outside of soldiering, he was competent only in one field, that of agriculture and not, I think, too competent in that. He had been owner and overseer of a landed estate, but I have the impression from hearing him talk about life in the old country that he spent much of his time hunting in the wildwood which occupied half of the estate, and fishing in the lovely waters that bordered it. Even in our prairie home in the Kansas wilderness the hunter remained strong in him. If buffalo and antelope were near, or the wild geese calling, planting or harvesting could wait, no matter what the season or the weather. As for fishing, the roily river which bordered our American homestead on three sides offered little temptation to one who had had at his very door in Sweden the most alluring of inland lakes. Yet the passion of the fisherman would not down. In the long winter evenings I have often seen him while away the hours weaving fishing nets and fashioning other fishing gear—like bees in the tropics storing up honey for a winter that never comes.

If I seem to be finding fault with my father, I do not mean it so. Indeed I have a sneaking admiration for this indulgence of his "unpractical" nature. I have always been fascinated by Robert Louis Stevenson's account of his visit to the paradoxical Nautical Club in Belgium, where members (business and professional men) foregathered to dismiss from their minds the "frivolities" of their economic pursuits and give themselves over to "serious" matters. Here, they told him, "*voyez vous, nous sommes serieux.*"

But to be "serious" in that sense in a world which is not ordered to our preferences soon or late plunges us into serious embarrassments. My father, as the responsible head of a large family, at the age of forty-seven, and with very limited means was in a heart-breaking situation. Insofar as he knew one thing better than another, he knew land and its uses. But he had lost his land and the hope of having any in the old country. There remained but one prospect: across the Atlantic free land beckoned friendlily. After our Civil War there was in Sweden what Selma Lagerlöf has called a veritable "America Fever." There was wave upon wave of migration to the "Promised Land," and in the year 1869 my people embarked upon their great adventure—hopefully and bravely, I imagine, though with no little misgiving as they broke with familiar and happy associations and faced an unknown, nebulous future in the New World.

How painful the wrench of leaving must have been I never realized until during our stay in Sweden, we visited Jahnslunda, the old home, some sixty miles west of Stockholm. A fair demesne, it is, half in trim tenant farms and half in wild forest, spits of the land reaching out like fingers into beautiful Lake Mälaren, Sweden's island-studded, inland sea. Life there goes on very much as when my parents directed it seventy years ago, but the Norlins are now a fading memory; not, however, a vanished memory, for when I introduced myself to the priest of the parish church nearby I found that the Norlin occupation was still vivid in his mind, although he was a later comer to the parish. When I told him who I was his eyes brimmed with tears and he embraced me as one who had strayed from home. He took us through the old church and showed us affectionately the family records of births and christenings and deaths there preserved, and he took us also into the churchyard where towered a huge granite slab proclaiming that here my ancestors are at rest.

To my surprise, I found myself choked with an emotion which I had never felt before—a warming sense of kinship, of belonging, as it were, to a tribe. That feeling was pressed upon me also by my blood relations in Stockholm: I knew little or nothing about them, but they knew of me and welcomed me with a cordiality which made me feel an ingrate. Family feeling and pride, which had been alien to me, were strong in them, and I might almost say that they took me in hand as if determined to fill out a gap in my education. They showed me pridefully the Swedish Family Register (*Svenska Slägt Kallender*) with its twenty pages devoted to the honorable part played by the Norlin clan in Swedish history. Also I was presented by an older cousin with an elaborate family tree which he had prepared with great research and care and written out in the finest of steel-engraving script at the age of seventy-six, without glasses, which I can barely read with benefit of oculists!

I have scanned these records of the Norlin lineage with some curiosity to see if I could discover any "gene" which might throw some light on what I have done with my life, but I have found little to my purpose. Something of my father's carelessness about money I suppose I have "come by honestly"; otherwise I should not have taken the vow of poverty so far as the great material prizes are concerned and entered upon an academic career. But only in the first "stem-father" (1702–1780) to bear the Norlin cognomen do I find any analogue to my pursuits. He distinguished himself as a student at the University of Uppsala, won his doctorate there with honors, became a scholar-pastor of the State Church and the head of a school. But here the rough parallel ceases; for the record closes with the words: "He was an extraordinary man, original and headstrong, which traits mark his descendants also."

The later bearers of the name, while submitting themselves to the educational processes of their time, show little interest in scholarly pursuits, following for the most part military or public careers, though one of my uncles, Elias, developed an interest in chemistry and physics after attaining the rank of major in the army and won the "high prize of the Swedish Academy of Science for discovering the atomic weight of iron."

On my mother's side, however—in the Fahnehjelm lineage, recorded in the Swedish Calendar of Nobility (the family was ennobled in 1647)—I find more devotion to letters, the arts, and scholarship. My mother was herself a very cultivated woman. Incidentally, she taught me my first French and German, and if I now pronounce these tongues with approximate correctness, it is because she set my vocal organs properly in my early childhood. Also she had a gift for writing and practiced it for publication. I am, I believe, more my mother's than my father's son.

3. The Kansas Frontier

I was born on April first (*absit omen*), in 1871, on the Kansas frontier, near what is now the flourishing town of Concordia. Concordia—what a name to roll upon the tongue!

I have puzzled much over many of the place names in our country and tried to imagine what "psychology" lay behind them. I mean those names which startle one by their inappropriateness. Some seem to have sprung from the sense of humor which delights in incongruities:

there is, for example, a mud pond in Colorado which is named Lake Como, and I have noted in arid regions a fondness for names ending in Wells or Springs. Other names seem to reflect either moods of levity or of grandiose expectations or both: Naples in Utah, Paris in Texas, Cairo in Illinois are typical cases in point. In fact, there are fourteen Cairos in the United States; Naples lends its name to eleven of our (mostly inland) hamlets; Paris to nineteen, London to ten, Brighton to twenty-four (not watering) places, Stockholm to six villages; Berlin to twenty one, the grandeur that was Rome to seventeen; and the glory that was Athens to twenty three!

Still other names seem to have had their birth in that passion for magniloquence which was a concomitant of our westward march, and among them I would place euphonious Concordia. Or is this only a half-truth? Is there, perhaps, hidden in this name and others like it a rainbow-dream of things longed for and hoped for in the future? An acute English observer of the American scene as it was in the middle of the last century, Alexander Barklay, wrote of our people that, unlike the peoples of the old world, they "exalt their heads to the skies in contemplation of what the grandeur of their country is to be. Others claim respect because of things done by a long line of ancestors: an American glories in the achievements of a distant posterity." This may be the inner truth of our high-sounding nomenclature. Nevertheless, Cocordia was a curious name with which to christen an inchoate and untamed region.

I have said that my mother had a gift for writing. She lived an *Odyssey*, what a pity she did not think to write it down! Such a record would have given us one of the most interesting documents of our pioneer history; and it would, I think, have been rather unique in that it would have set forth the story of a family, not inured to hardship, but soft from comfortable, servant-tended living, plunged suddenly and unpreparedly into the privations, hardships, and rigors of a wilderness existence.

But that story is buried in oblivion, and I am not able to bring it to life. Two years of the pioneer struggle had passed before I was born, and some four years must have come and gone before I could have any memorable impression of it. The fragments that are preserved in my recollections—and there are few—are such as stamped themselves indelibly on my memory in early childhood, whether from talk of my elders or from my own, later, experiences.

It seems at first thought beyond belief that my father (his will was law in our household) with such a family—my mother delicately nurtured, a flock of children ranging from seventeen years of age to a babe in arms—should have resolved to risk their future away from ordered settlements and even at first beyond the protection of the Stars and Stripes rather than to settle somewhere in the middle states (Illinois or Iowa, for example), where civilization was at least on the way and life was comparatively secure and land was still to be had at low cost. Manifestly his choice was reckless and imprudent. But prudence was less in his nature than the spirit of adventure. The frontier beckoned to him with the promise of free land, the lure of the unknown, and the call to the sportsman of wild game in abundance.

In the early spring of 1869, my people reached Junction City in eastern Kansas, which was then the end of the railroad and the verge of civilization. There he left my mother and the younger children and, taking his older sons with him, proceeded to spy out the land further west. A stout covered wagon drawn by mules and loaded heavily with farm implements and tools, seeds for planting, and the necessary food supplies was the means of transportation.

Fortunately for the expedition, he was able to employ as guides and helpers two Swedish adventurers who were well acquainted with the country. One was a veritable giant named Boberg, a happy-go-lucky, ready-for-anything sort of man, who had roughed it as a hunter in India and Africa and was now courting excitement in the Wild West. The other, no less competent and a bit more steady, was a younger man named Halvorsen. Without their help, I fear the venture would have been disastrous.

They explored the country to a point some hundred miles west of Junction City in the valley of the Republican River, where they camped and began to make ready for our home that was to be. But they had only gone so far in seizing possession of the land as to improvise a blockhouse for their temporary shelter and protection when the wilderness pounced upon them with a snarl. One day, the meat supply having given out, my father with Boberg had gone off on a buffalo hunt, leaving the boys behind with Halvorsen to look after them. The boys were playing along the river, when they spied a band of Indians circling the cabin. They had dug out for themselves in play a secret cave in the river bank, and now they rushed to this refuge and hid themselves away therein, not daring to venture forth until at evening they heard their father's voice calling them desperately. The cabin was a ruin of smouldering coals; and Halvorsen lay dead upon the grass, his body riddled with arrows and his scalp torn off.

"Welcome each rebuff," says the poet of valorous living. With what welcome they took this blow, I can only surmise. The cabin could be rebuilt, but the loss of Halvorsen could ill be repaired. A few weeks later, Boberg, carelessly stooping down to discover the cause of a movement in the grass, was struck in the throat by a rattlesnake, and lived but a few hours. These were the first white men to rest in peace on our Kansas homestead, and the spot where they were laid became our burial ground.

Hardly had Halvorsen been placed in his rude coffin and buried, my father reading the burial service from the prayerbook which he carried with him, than tidings came of another tragedy. The nearest neighbors then lived ten miles away. The same band of Indians had raided them; and my father, notwithstanding his own desperate case, headed a party to see what damage had been done and to lend a hand. But there was nothing left to do for the White family except to bury with Christian rites the terribly mutilated bodies of the father and mother and two sons, the two daughters having been carried off into captivity.

That was happily the end of Indian depredations in that region. News of the Indian raids had somehow been raced to Fort Riley, the nearest military post, and within a few days Captain Custer and his cavalry had pegged their hundred tents where our first cabin lay in ashes, and later they administered to the savages so cruel a lesson that they never troubled our neighborhood again.

The fear of Indians removed, my father's party set to work with a will to build a home and make the first beginnings of a farm. A house of logs was carefully and sturdily built from timber that grew in abundance by the riverside. My father *would* have a house, which was a bit "highhat," since the human habitations which were in fashion on that frontier were little more than caves excavated in sharply sloping hillsides ("dugouts" they were called) with wooden fronts to provide a window and a door. But we had a "dugout" too, in which my brothers slept, the house being not large enough to accommodate so large a family.

It was in this house that I was born, and I remember it well as it was when I became aware of my surroundings. There were windows of glass—a luxury on the early frontier, but there were no screens of defense against flies, which pestered us at meal times in the summer, or against hosts of mosquitos, which were so avid to live to the full "their one crowded hour of glorious life" that they often drove us out of doors to make a stand in the smoke of smudge fires—a smother which choked the besieged only less than the besiegers. The roof of the house was of sod, which was not entirely proof against heavy, long-continued rains, but this defect was compensated for by its blossoming out gaily with wild flowers in late spring and early summer. The floor, and this I recall with rather painful vividness, was of hewn cottonwood planks which, not too smooth when laid, became badly warped from repeated scrubbings and made rough and perilous going for a child learning his first steps. The furnishings, it can be imagined, were primitive and meagre. I recall a festal occasion, though I do not remember what the occasion was, when the neighbors from the countryside came together at our house. Preparations had been made for abundant feasting. A long table, extending from end to end of our living room, had been improvised by laying rough boards precariously on kegs and boxes. The table groaned with such food as the farm afforded. But in the midst of the feasting, its equilibrium was upset and the dishes crashed into fragments on the floor. It must have spoiled the party, though as to this my mind is vacant. What left a scar upon my memory was the humiliation of having to drink for weeks out of a tin can. It was not easy to run out a hundred miles to Junction City for a cup!

But I outrun my story. The house being furnished, they made the first advance towards the taming of the land. Part of the wild prairie was broken and in the overturned sod such crops were planted as could mature in a single season: potatoes and other vegetables; sorghum, to take the place of sugar; and, above all, corn—corn being then the staff of life, and the drink too; for, when parched, ground and boiled, it furnished a standard beverage when coffee and tea were hard to come by. The "white-bread days" were in the future and so were milk and butter; for the only cows to be had in that locality in the earliest pioneering days were of the Texas "long-horn" breed and were about as docile as the buffaloes. My father tried to milk one of these wild creatures, but was savagely set upon by her, narrowly escaping with his life.

It was now early summer: the crops were growing lustily, the season was at its height, and the time auspicious for the reunion of the family. Home came my mother and the four younger children—not a very happy homecoming, for in my mother's arms was the lifeless body of her youngest child, who during the four-days journey from Junction City in a jolting wagon had sickened and died on the way. And little Annie sleeps the long sleep by Halvorsen and Boberg, the guides who had in a manner demarked her destiny.

With what zest (or lack of zest) my mother entered upon and accustomed herself to the life in the new home, unhappily I do not know. I do know that the first Christmas season stood out in drab contrast to that festival of good cheer which the Scandinavians are wont to celebrate with more zeal and devotion than any other people of the Christian world.

As the season approached in the wilderness, the food supply in the household having run low, my father set out for Junction City to replenish the larder and to buy such other things as would help to make a "Happy Christmas." It was good weather when he started—like a day in spring—but while he was on the return journey the mercury took a sudden dive and a blinding blizzard swept over the land. It was not safe to venture even from the house to the nearby stable without a line of rope, so easily could one be lost. A neighbor made the fatal mistake of braving the storm, and his body, buried in a drift, was not discovered until the following spring. Christmas came, but not my father. The household was overwhelmed with anxiety; my mother fell ill from the terrible suspense; and when my father returned safe and sound a few days later, having taken refuge in a farmstead by the way before the full fury of the storm broke upon him, he found her mourning for him as for one lost beyond hope.

These not too cheerful episodes, which I have picked from the memory of those who had a part in them, would seem to indicate that the early days on the frontier were days of "dangerous" living. The first years were, no doubt, the hardest; but the struggle with the wilderness was rather long drawn out as I, myself, can testify. I recall as if it were yesterday a bright morning when, playing out of doors, I noticed suddenly a darkening of the sun as if in eclipse. What happened was that the sunlight was dimly trickling through a huge, dense cloud of grasshoppers—billions upon billions of them—that swooped down upon the land, swarming, crawling, and devouring every green and growing thing—the new-born crops, the lush grass of spring, even the leaves and their stems upon the trees. Before the day was done, the farm was a desert and a desolation. That was the great scourge of 1875. There were others, though not so devastating; but for years anxious eyes were turned from springing crops into the sun, fearing to see the tiny specks which were the advance guards of a noxious horde.

What this visitation meant to my elders I can now well imagine. But I must confess that a six-year-old boy, in company with other irrational creatures (particularly the gizzard tribes), found all this intensely diverting and exciting. The barnyard fowls—chickens and turkeys—had the time of their lives; joy-maddened by this manna fallen from the heavens, they gorged themselves upon it to more than repletion. One old turkey gobbler carried his greed to such an extreme (those will please take note who lay bare the mysteries of the human soul by the revelations of animal behavior) that he suffered an acute neurosis, being baffled and frustrated because every time he snapped up one luscious insect another escaped from his overcrowded gullet!

I recall as vividly another time which was equally disastrous and, to me, equally diverting. It must have been at the high tide of summer, for the wheat was in shock upon the yellow stubble and the corn was tall enough for me to hide in. In the middle of the night I was dragged roughly out of bed to find myself standing knee-deep in water. It had rained heavily for days and the overflowing river was turning our valley into a vast lake. We barely escaped with our lives to an upland farm and thence beheld our house sink like a wrecked ship and disappear beneath the rising flood. When the waters had subsided the livestock and the shocks of wheat had been swept away, but the house stood firm, and the corn survived, though bent and staggering from the struggle and crusted, as was everything, with slimy mud.

Naturally, the events which engraved themselves sharply on my memory and are here written down are the dark shadows of this adventuring and not the brighter colors which must have relieved them. I have heard my mother remark that the early days of grappling with the frontier were the happiest days of her life—a testimony which I never cease to marvel at. How could my people, with a background of the manner of life which they had exchanged for this, have stuck it out? Perhaps it was because there was no other door of escape than that which opened on the future; or perhaps there was in the struggle a saving grace of buoyancy which we who have been softened by the ministry of gadgets and easements lack the imagination to recapture.

An excellent reporter* of the rigors of another frontier explains in the form of a western parable why the early settlers refused to be driven out by one calamity after another:

A cowboy, trying to control a wild steer by holding him by the tail, was jerked off his feet and dragged headlong over the plain, his clothing stripped and his skin torn by cactus and thorn bushes, when another cowboy rode up yelling: "You fool, why the hell don't you let go?" "Let go? How *can* I let go? It's all I can do to hang on," came the weak but resolute reply.

That explanation is engaging, though "hanging on" is not, I think, the whole story. The frontier life was marked most of all by the absence of defeatism. No days were completely black—without some glimmer of reassurance. If those who battled through them did not

---

*Mrs. Cole, in *The Land of the Burnt Thighs.*

exactly "welcome each rebuff" or "greet the unseen with a cheer," they were possessed by a resiliency and hopefulness which lifted them over the roughest places.

Much has been written about the "down-drag of the wilderness," and with reason, but I cannot testify to it from my experience. We were poor but so were the others. There was no envy. We were all equal in what we did not have. If I were to compare the deprivations of my boyhood with what youngsters now require or have thrust upon them, I should point a contrast so extreme that it might constrain to pity for my lack of almost everything they have. But the pity would be misplaced; perhaps it is I who had the better fortune. A philosopher of ancient times once dared the paradox that the greatest good fortune lies, not in having the most possessions, but in having the fewest wants. In the face of a more modern and popular philosophy, which makes happiness consist in a wealth of teeming appetites and a plethora of satieties, such an ideal seems, no doubt, naive. Nevertheless there is this much to be said for it in my own case that my deprivations did not blunt but, rather, whetted the edge of a hunger to explore the world and what it had in store.

There was no church in our vicinity, but religion was brought more intimately to us by visiting clergymen who preached, not to congregations, but to informal gatherings of neighbors at our home. The services were of the Baptist sect. My people in Sweden had been for generations adherents of the State (Lutheran) Church. Why my parents changed, I can only conjecture. Perhaps it was felt that the old church was too formal, too easygoing—too aware that human beings are not simply disembodied spirits and, therefore, overlenient—and that a more strenuous and exacting evangel was more in keeping with their precarious struggle in the new world.

However that may be, strict family devotions were so much a part of our daily routine that we were not allowed to forget that we were living *sub specie aeternitatis*. Two of my brothers (I am the youngest son) felt called to the ministry and one of them studied theology and qualified to be a clergyman. I, however, was never deeply affected by religious rituals or exhortations. Only once in my life have I had what I may term a mystical experience, and that was in my childhood. I was quite alone and subject to no extraneous excitement, when suddenly and for no explicable (except by Freudian's) reason I was possessed by an ecstacy—a sense of being lifted up and borne along on wings out of myself and all earthly bonds. It was so strange and extraordinary that I went to my mother for an explanation of its meaning. She made no comment, but embraced me, her eyes brimming with glad tears, as if she knew that underneath me I had felt the "everlasting arms . . ."

That was unique and I have never experienced the like again. "Revivals" and their mystical exaltations have always left me cold and, I must add, with an uncomfortable feeling of being left out. Why was I denied the warming comfort of what seemed to be a quite common and normal experience? Was I a lost sheep? To this day I wonder at the mystics, who are unquestionably convinced of realities which seem unreal to those of us who have no part in them. Have they some truth that we have missed?

At any rate, I hold in reverence the faith and worship that pervaded my boyhood home. Indeed I have never felt like scoffing at any form of sincere religion. I cannot but envy all those who feel assured that they have a rock of refuge in a definite corpus of belief. If they find in any Credo an anodyne against the blows of circumstance (*procial abeste Marxisti*!); if religion is, as Monsieur

Jaures defined it to be, "the cradle in which have been rocked the sorrows of this earth"; if it is a rod and staff giving comfort and assurance even in the valley of death; and if, besides, it sounds a bugle call to brave and fruitful living; then I am impelled to say with Matthew Arnold: "For God's sake believe it then!" For, "where is the way where light dwelleth?" As to myself, however, religion has never meant anything confined in sect or creed but simply a sense of being allied, as Wordsworth felt, with the Nature of Things—of being, when truest to myself, in accord with a Power that struggles endlessly with us to bring peace and order out of the tumults and chaos of our existence. Or is that, too, a mysticism?

When I was of school age, there was a country school within walking distance of our farm. To this in term time (which was all too short) I trudged a mile and a half each day, no matter what the weather. Even when my parents thought it better for me to stay at home, I commonly persuaded them to let me go; for it was "fun" to be in school, and interesting. It was, naturally, the more entertaining and interesting since there was so little to distract us from this interest—no stadium frenzies, no movie thrills, no whizzing in motor cars, no wild parties or midnight dances, no fever of rushing from one excitement to another.

The school itself was, I need not say, very primitive in its appointments. It was a one-room affair, barely furnished with a stove, a water pail in one corner, rude benches for the "scholars" (pupils were "scholars" then), an equally rude desk for the teacher, and a black board. There was no library, not even a dictionary, nor was the teacher any great store-house of knowledge. I recall being fascinated by the melodious and mouth-filling word *hieroglyphic* in the formidable column of five-syllabled words on the last page of our spelling book. Such a word, out of the past, is taboo today in building up the vocabulary of youth as having no utility in a living present, but it interested me, and I asked the teacher what it meant. The teacher did not know. My mother knew, but only enough to whet my curiosity. Later when I had access to an encyclopedia, that one haunting word opened up to me the fascinations of ancient civilizations and stirred in me an interest which eventually had something to do with my devotion to specialized studies in that field.

This and other experiences lead me to question the now-common shibboleth that in our educational policy we should proceed always from the familiar to the unfamiliar, from the immediate to the remote, from our own backyards to the backyards of the world, from the present to the past, from the nickelodeon weekly to the homeric epic, *und so weiter*. At any rate, I reversed the process, and there may be something in the idea that "distance lends enchantment" to the student. One might shock the pedagogists further by clinging to the superstition that we can best approach an understanding of the present with some background of knowledge of the sweep of the centuries which have left us where we are.

But to return to the frontier school. The teacher had her hands more than full. She (male teachers were rare) had to know the subjects insofar as they were covered by the textbooks then in use. From nine o'clock in the morning until noon and from one o'clock until four in the afternoon she heard recitations continuously save for two fifteen-minute recesses, some of the "scholars" being called front to recite their lessons, while others conned their texts in preparation for their turn. There were frequent interruptions. Hands were raised and fingers snapped, now here now there. "Please, teacher, how is this word pronounced?" or "Please, may I get a drink?" or "Please, may I go out?" etc.

Naturally, the teacher had to be, if not a scholastic authority, a patient and resourceful person, and that at a time when teachers were born, not factory made. Above all, discipline had to be preserved, this being a primary consideration. A school board seeking a teacher required not so much a paragon of learning as a disciplinarian who could preserve order and maintain authority. There was no thought as yet of letting the child flower spontaneously without direction—without weeding, without cultivation, without pruning, without discipline. Even corporal punishment was taken for granted as a good thing. But discipline was meted out for derelictions from standards of good behavior, not for mental shortcomings. There was no "dunce cap" or "being stood in the corner" for the humiliation of dullards, nor did any bundle of rods (fasces) stand behind the teacher's desk to symbolize to the learners the fearful purpose of their education. So far we were advanced from the more or less fabled barbarisms of an earlier day.

But, on the other hand, there was no prejudice whatsoever against putting a premium upon scholastic excellence and so stimulating intellectual endeavor. On the contrary, competiton and emulation were encouraged. We were permitted and liked to show off in our recitations what we had learned from our books; we liked to compete for scholastic standings; ribbons were won and pinned to our coats. Outside of the class routine there were "exhibitions" and contests of various sorts. "Spelling down," for example, was a frequent exercise which all seemed to enjoy, even those who went down first. No one had as yet hit upon the "inferiority complex" and made the avoidance of it a controlling principle of public education. The period of enlightenment had not dawned with its insistence on "democracy" in education—a hybrid humanitarianism which permits distinctions and emulations in dress and promotes by all discoverable encitements—dinners, rallies, pageants, emoluments and prizes—emulations and distinctions on the athletic field and in other "student activities," but does not signalize at all any distinction in the scholastic activities which it is the primary business of the school to promote, regarding it as the sin against the Holy Ghost to allow any rivalry in this province or to tolerate any recognition of intellectual achievement lest those who lag behind be undone by a sense of frustration and defeatism; the result being that all pupils, regardless of what they do or do not do in their studies, are not only kept religiously in school (as in an amiable sanitarium) but moved from grade to grade in happy companionship with their age-fellows until duly diplomatized and proclaimed to the world as having enjoyed for a term of years a regimen of felicitous and unalloyed equality. This represents, manifestly, a sharp departure from Jefferson's idea of public education in a democracy as a means of discovering and singling out the best minds and training them adequately for service to the state. But Jefferson lived long ago. *Autres temps, autres moeurs.* Why should his ghost haunt us now?

As for my country school it was, as I have pointed out, primitive, or should I say mediaeval? No educationist bureaucrat of this day would "accredit" it in any particular. He would pronounce the physical entourage impossible, the curriculum "barren," and the teaching "inefficient." Yet my recollections of it are unclouded by any sense of lack or any feeling of resentment. I do not recall whether my teachers were "stimulating" or not. They were there to keep order and hear me recite. I learned from my textbooks and in that learning I felt myself growing pleasurably in an expanding world which they opened up to me. I recall with special gratitude the "readers," which introduced me to the enchantments of literary expression. I had not even heard of Keats' sonnet *On First Looking Into Chapman's Homer*, but new planets were beginning to sweep into my ken.

There was, as has been implied, a dearth of books on the frontier. Those who journeyed into the wilderness were over-freighted with other necessities than libraries; and after they had settled in it they lacked for many years the means of purchasing them. Here somewhat reluctantly I relate an incident which, though it stands out like a mountain peak in my boyhood, will likely seem unreal and trivial to any who have been blest (or cursed) with surfeit. The incident has to do with the first novel that ever fell into my hands. How I came by it, what its title was, what the story was—everything but its blue binding and the enticing picture that was stamped upon the cover—have faded from my memory. But I have not forgotten the effect upon me of the reading of it. It chanced that it came into my possession at a very unopportune time to indulge my wild curiosity about it; for I had been told to watch some cattle that afternoon and keep them in the grass pasture and away from the corn. What to do? There was a moral struggle, which ended in my taking the book along. I herded the cattle into the pasture and sat down in the deep grass to have a look at my treasure. I began to read; I forgot the cattle; I had rubbed Aladdin's lamp and was transported into a world of enchantment. I was supremely happy.

The cattle, left to their own volition, strayed into the cornfield and did great damage to the crop; and I was soundly whipped, as I deserved, but no punishment could quench the joy of that transgression.

I would give a good deal to be able to recover that book, even though I could not hope to recapture the mood which it inspired. I am sure that it was a very romantic picture of a nobility which our critics for some years now have been relegating to the limbo of unrealities. If I were to read it today, I fear that I should find it impossible to imagine why it was that under its spell I felt exalted and raised in stature. The writers who abhor to brace us with the wine of life as if they were divinely anointed to preoccupy us with its dregs have spoiled us for such reading, though I cannot help wondering whether they have not despoiled us too. Is there not now between the impossibly noble and the impossibly ignoble a no-man's land which begs to be occupied by a literature that would envisage the realities of human dignity and worth and help us to rise above what the French have called our *nostalgie pour la soul la boue*?

Perhaps this very question may be romantic and vacuous; but my highly esteemed friend, Howard Mumford Jones, than whom no one has a sharper eye to see through all cant and sham, has at this writing published a plea for a more tonic literature under the title "*Nobility Wanted*"!

It may be pertinent in the story of my early education for me to say (or should I confess?) that discipline was a by no means insignificant factor in my bringing up, not in school only but at home as well. My father was rather stern and strict and, though my mother was a gentling influence, there was a somewhat rigorous, not to say puritanic, regimen in our household. There was a very definite moral code, and I was so unenlightened that I did not question the rightness of its imperatives nor the justice of being rebuked or otherwise disciplined for infractions of them. I was not obsessed by any fear of punishment. If I stepped out of bounds, I expected and stood ready to pay the price. It all seemed fair enough.

In saying this, I will be accused of romanticizing. A new philosophy has seized the minds of men. I ought to run true to form and confess to a desperate sense of bafflement and frustration because my native impulses in boyhood were not encouraged to stray beyond the bounds of decorum. But I can testify to no such experience, and I cannot but wonder whether a doctrine, which is, no doubt, useful in the therapy of sick souls, is of such universal validity that all must live by it. At any rate; I had as much fun and I believe more fun than those youngsters who feel immune from any set of commandments and free to indulge their every urge and whim and vagary to the point of repletion and boredom. Inhibition—awful word—is now the dread dragon that wounds and stultifies our personalities. Yet I make bold to say that we suffer less from inhibitions than from the lack of them. Moral imperatives are like blazed trails which we can travel undistractedly; if they be lacking, we are lost in the woods, bewildered, baffled, and frantic to find someone to tell us where to go and ready to listen to any Hitler—any charlatan—who will blithly tell us that he is the way and will order us to march therein.

But are there moral imperatives any more? Our revolutionaries tell us that morals like everything else are in a state of flux. "All things are flowing: nothing abides." An irresistible tide carries the wreckage of all things that have been. That may be true of taboos, but is it true of morals? Are honesty, truthfulness, temperance, patience, sympathy, magnanimity, love no longer fixed stars by which we must get our bearings and set our courses or suffer shipwreck in our lives? How long must we suffer fools gladly?

4. We Move To Wisconsin

Stevenson has remarked somewhere, I think in commenting on the restlessness behind western migrations, "that to travel hopefully is a better thing than to arrive." By the time I was eleven years of age, we had "arrived." The region was now fairly settled. The railroad had come and brought us into touch with the outside world. It was no longer necessary to travel by wagon for days, going and coming, for supplies; these could be had in the nearby town. The crops in the earlier days were of value only as they could be consumed on the farm—food for the household and for the animals. Sometimes as in the case of a surplus of corn it was used for fuel, there being no better use to put it to. But with the coming of the railroad, the crops had a market, and we became moderately prosperous.

But the adventuring was over; the wilderness was conquered; the victory grew stale; life had settled into a tame, unexciting routine. My parents became restive, especially my father. He was not content to drag out the remainder of his life on the Kansas prairie. The rainbow's end was not there but somewhere else. Besides, the sea was in his blood and he wanted to get back to water again. He had found a spot after his heart's desire on the Wisconsin peninsula on the beautiful eastern shore of Green Bay. He sold our Kansas farm, purchased land adjoining a little village, then a remote fishing and lumbering hamlet, now a flourishing summer resort; and in the early summer of 1882 we were installed in our new, Wisconsin home.

The four years following our migration from Kansas stand out as the golden age of my boyhood—my heaven on earth. Indeed if I had to lay down specifications for a New Jerusalem, I could not improve upon my surroundings in that happy period, provided I could include the youthful zest I had in them.

I have always been impressed by the poverty of our conventional imaginings about Kingdom Come. Even the lustrous home of the blessed pictured in the apocalypse of our Christian tradition, with its streets of gold, its walls of jasper, its splendor of precious stones, its unremitting noon-day glare—no night, no moon or stars, no dawn or sunset, and no sea—has seemed to me a marvel to gaze at for a time, Baedeker in hand, but not a place to live in. Better the heaven of *Green Pastures*, where there is at least a river with good fishing! Should there be in store for us an unearthly heaven worthy of the name, I am sure there must be fishing in it.

Well, in the lovely waters of Green Bay there was fishing galore. At evening the red-winged fishing boats came sailing into the harbor with their rich hauls of trout and bass and whitefish and sturgeon; at least one day out of the seven, my father and I trolled for bass or trout over the shoal waters of a flock of islands within rowing distance of the mainland; and almost any day in the season I could fish from the village dock and bring home perch enough to feed the family.

It was then a fisherman's paradise, and that meant much to me, who to this day regard angling as one of the chief ends of man which Calvin, strangely, overlooked. But besides fishing there were rowing and sailing and swimming and leaping from back to back of the great logs impounded in huge rafts to be fed in due time to the screaming teeth of the sawmill of the village. For much of the summer I was on the water or in it; and from this time dates my distinctive proficiency in swimming, this being the one form of athletics in which I have excelled.

The fall too was not without its enchantments of

Fifteen or sixteen years old

hunting squirrels and partridges (big game was for men) and of gathering nuts when the wildwood was reluctantly letting go its glory of crimson and gold to flutter about and strew the ground with riotous color.

Winter was a long season of battle against rigorous weather. To some, no doubt, it was a siege to be endured. I remember my mother dreaded its "aid and comfort" to a pulmonary weakness from which she was never entirely free. But for me it ushered in a new and exciting change. From the coming of the first snow in November, we did not see the ground for some four months. Indeed at times our "worm fences" disappeared completely beneath a deep, vast sea of white, over which one could skim on skis or snowshoes without let or hindrance anywhere. Our manner of life was revolutionized. All wheeled vehicles were put away in the barns for a long vacation to be replaced with all manner of gliding mechanisms—cutters, bob-sleighs, hand-sleds, skates and skis—which could minister to winter's work or play. The house was "banked" to withstand the cold. Wood for fuel was piled high at the gate. Cotton garments, hats, and shoes were discarded for heavy woolens and caps and felt stockings and boots or heavy moccasins. Many, particularly the lumbermen (for deep winter was the time when the axes rang in the forest), wore "mackinaw" suits of garish hues, often contrasting hues, mostly scarlet and blue. It was not uncommon for a man to be decked out in a green tasseled cap or pull-over, a scarlet jacket, breeches of vivid blue, yellow leggins, and tan-colored moccasins. These multicolored men passed our house each day and gave a touch of picturesque variety to our white-clad world.

As I have said, the coming of winter was hailed by me as a glorious birth, but none the less welcome was the relaxing of its long hard grip, in March or early April:

the boom, boom, boom of the ice breaking up in the bay, the tinkle of melting snow by the roadside, the good fun of collecting in pails the drip, drip of thawing maples about the sugar camp, the feeding of fires under the huge kettles in which the sap was boiled down to its residue of syrup or sugar—all this with a sense of the rising tide of life within oneself, responding to the first stirrings of the resurrection of all growing things, though the soft air was still a bit brisk with the retreating frost and the gaunt trees seemed not to know just what to do as they looked down on patches of snow still telling of winter and sprays of the pink arbutus telling of spring. It was I think a marvellous place for a boy to grow up in.

I pen what I have written as if these years were an uninterrupted playtime. It is only natural that the brightest colors remain most vivid in my mind. But there were other things, and among them school. But my school experience during the period is rather misty in my recollections. Certainly it did not mean to me what it had meant in the country school in Kansas where I hailed the opening of the term with enthusiasm and its close with genuine regret. There, going to school was more interesting than anything else, here it meant being shut in from the allurements of the out of doors. I still felt that books were magic casements through which I would one day envisage the fullness of life and penetrate its mysteries, and I not only did not neglect my studies but read avidly whatever I could lay my hands on. Yet my eyes were ever and anon straying to the windows to glimpse the world outside, and the close of the term brought something of a sense of relief from imprisonment.

This was in no sense, I think, the fault of the teachers, who were, I thought, the unwilling instruments of our incarceration. One teacher in particular we adored. She was a rather small and pretty thing who seemed little older than ourselves; and thereby hangs a tale. One day the keeper of the lighthouse near by, a gaunt and forbidding woman, broke into our session and proceeded to berate the teacher in very violent language for the latter's treatment of her child. Under this scathing attack, the teacher broke down utterly with chagrin and anger and could not say a word. The tirade went on, the tension grew. Finally, not able to contain myself any longer, I rushed from my desk, confronted the virago and shouted in her face, "Get out, get out!" I expected her to set upon me, but to my surprise and great relief she did get out. That episode gave me a distinction among my schoolmates such as I have never enjoyed before or since, and I must confess to a feeling for a time that there was more than one St. George in world history.

Also I was at an age when I was beginning to be useful on the farm, and I was put to work at many a tedious chore. I was not averse to work, but it seemed to me that the tasks I was put to were unworthy, being such things as grown men would not be demeaned by. Plying the axe or holding the plow or swinging the scythe or driving the horses or other work which the men monopolized seemed noble occupations, whereas to poor me were relegated such jobs as picking up and carrying off the stones which were turned up at every ploughing from the limestone strata that underlay our shallow soil, gathering and piling up brush wood for burning where the men were clearing land, weeding by hand—a slow and backbreaking business—and, most degrading of all, picking potato-bugs and other vermin from the growing plants.

In my heart I rebelled against such occupations as in a manner a slavery imposed upon my youthfulness, and I longed to grow quickly into manhood and so into the freedom to do things worthwhile.

I am here only recording faithfully a boy's mind at the time, and not voicing a just complaint. In fact, my mother and father were very considerate of me. Here it may have some pertinence to confess to something which has been on my conscience through the years. One day when I was helping the men in clearing a bit of land in the forest, I became intolerably hungry. It was an hour till lunch time, but I could not wait. Unhappily I spied a fresh plug of chewing tobacco in the pocket of a vest hanging on a stump near by. It looked good; it tasted good. I swallowed a mouthful and presently was very sick. Soon after I was found, more dead than alive and wanting to die, and was put in a wagon and hurried home. My mother scolded my father for not realizing that I was too young and delicate for such work. He assented, though somewhat doubtfully, and to my discomfort. I wanted to come out with the truth, but I was too ashamed to do so; and I was set free to do what I liked for the rest of that summer, though my father must have been puzzled by the zest and vigor I had in doing what I liked. Suffice it to say that the work which I did on the farm, however dull and irksome, was, no doubt, good for me if only because it sharpened the edge of my response to the beauty which surrounded me on every side.

If my response to that beauty should seem at all extravagant, it must be remembered that I came to it from the comparative drabness of a prairie environment. Not that I consciously made any comparison. Only dimly and vaguely I began to realize the part that natural beauty could play in one's life, though such words as beauty and beautiful were not among my vocables at the time. I can only be sure that from the first day in my new surroundings I was flooded with a sense of well-being; something had gone to my head like strong wine, and I was strangely happy.

I despair of being able to convey this feeling adequately to anyone. I have tried to do so for myself in an autobiographical poem which I have called *Beauty*, and perhaps I can do no better than to repeat some lines of it here.

Our new, northern home where wood and waters met;
A rambling house, brown weathered by the sun,
Built high upon a hillside for the view,
Or to be neighbor to a goodly spring
That welled forth there through the rifted rock;
Hard by tall lilacs bloomed, sweetening the air,
And at a little distance one could see
A rose-green mist of burgeoning apple trees.

Beyond the house, upland forest, mile on mile,
Age-old, inviolate, magnificent;
Armies of cedar, hemlock, balsam, fir,
Maple, ironwood, beech and, loveliest of all,
White-armored companies of slender birch.

To left and right, like arms stretched out to sea,
Were limestone cliffs, deep-stained with age;
On one a lighthouse warned of peril there
Where dark waves whitened over hidden rocks.

In front, below, where sea gulls caught the sun,
There flashed the emerald surface of the bay,
Receding boundlessly, or so I thought,
Save for a broken chain of wooded islands
That seemed to lie asleep in quiet weather,
But were alert to ward off angry storms
And make a friendly harborage within.

Beyond the islands, far as eye could reach,
One saw the outspread wings of fishing boats
And of high-masted ships.

O wondrous world, my first apocalypse!
Other times I have come near that ecstasy:
Once when first I glimpsed the Rocky Mountains,
That were to be my sentinels of home;

Once when in Sicily I felt the charm
Of Taormina, high upon her garden terrace
Between the mountains and the midmost sea,
Serene and smiling amidst her oranges
And oleanders, save where the white cone
Of untamed Aetna belched forth fire and smoke;
And once again when, nearing dark Tahiti,
I saw the jewelled fingers of awakening dawn
Reach up and touch with sapphire the peak of Diadem,
Above the flames of poinciana trees.

Yet never any scene has fired my senses
As that which first revealed to youthful eyes
The beauty and the splendor of this earth.

Am I romanticising about a boyhood fifty years removed from this writing? It would not be surprising if I were. No one can be really human who does not have in his heart some golden age of the past or of the future. But I have revisited again and again the scenes which I have attempted to describe, and always without disillusionment. Changes, not to my liking, have taken place. The sails are gone and the primeval woods are gone. Fenced in summer homes have occupied the ground over which I roamed without let or hindrance as a boy. But the lovely bay is unpreempted and unspoiled; the picturesque cliffs are a bit more mellowed by time but otherwise unchanged; and a second growth of forest here and there springs hopefully over the graves of ancient ancestors in whose twilight shade I sometimes lost my way long ago: and whenever I go back I am able to recapture the strong, if nebulous, emotion that stirred me in my youth.

·II·

PRESIDENTIAL YEARS

President Norlin always had a strong interest in college athletics, perhaps a reflection of the ancient Greek belief in a sound mind in a sound body. He was an expert on the tennis court and at the billiards table, a good mountain climber, and a fair amateur boxer who often got into the ring with his students. He was also an enthusiastic fisherman. As late as 1940 he fished the North St. Vrain River—with the aid of a cane.

As faculty representative to the Rocky Mountain Athletic Conference, Norlin learned a great deal about the virtues and the vices of intercollegiate sports. Later, during the 1920s and the 1930s, when he was chairman of the University Athletic Board, he did much to eliminate excessive abuses. His views of the proper role of sports in colleges and universities were solidly founded on his practical experience as a participant, an interested spectator, and an administrator.

THE PROPER ROLE OF COLLEGE ATHLETICS

Shortly after Thanksgiving, according to the Associated Press, the students of a state university to the west of us met to discuss a proposition made by an outside group which was organized into a "Boosters Club" for the promotion of "bigger and better" football teams. This "Boosters Club" had proposed to raise a very considerable fund in order to supplement the salary of the coach and to supply "athletic scholarships."

There was nothing very extraordinary in this situation. Such proposals have been made in other educational centers and accepted by educational institutions apparently with gratitude, at any rate with no manifest reluctance thus to surrender largely the control of athletic policy to outside fans. But the extraordinary fact in this case was that the students voted unanimously to reject the proposition.

And yet what happened the other day at the University of Nevada is growing less extraordinary among students; and I know of nothing more interesting or more encouraging in the collegiate world of recent years than such protests among the students themselves against tendencies and practices which are obviously professionalizing college athletics and yet appear to be tolerated and winked at by educational authorities.

I do not suppose that such protestations among the students are the expression of any toplofty idealism. I suppose, rather, that they express simply a downright feeling on their part that the colleges should not be crooked, that they should, in the promotion of athletics as in all other things, be straight and above board, and that above all they should not tolerate a situation where the college preaches one thing and permits groups within it or outside of it to practice another under the college flag.

We must all of us, students, faculties, alumni, and governing boards,—we must all of us face the fact that in our efforts to carry out an honest policy we are dealing with a very difficult problem, to some minds an impossible problem. The interest in intercollegiate contests is so tremendous, it organizes itself into forces that are so powerful, it expresses itself in storms of emotion which are so hard to stand up against, that some of us throw up our hands and let the winds carry us whither they list.

But to my mind the question is too vital to be dismissed in any such spirit of helplessness. To my mind—and I think you will agree with me—a college or university which allows itself to be dishonest merely because it is very difficult to go straight has lost its reason for existence. We in the colleges are expected, and rightly expected, in all that we do to have a sound influence upon the character of youth. But how can we do that? None of us will, I suppose, admit that we are not straight. On the contrary, we talk unctuously about the ideals fostered by athletics—their good effect upon character, the discipline which they afford in self-control, in good sportsmanship, and so on; and we even set up, or we assent to, elaborate laws and rules to keep them clean. But when we passively permit the clamor of the fans, insistent upon a Roman spectacle, to speak to the coach and to the management in language more convincing than our own lip service to ideals, saying to them almost in so many words, "get us a team; there are rules to be reckoned with, but rules or no rules, somehow, by hook or crook, get us a championship!"—when we permit that, I ask, are we honestly doing the job?

The other way of being honest is perhaps more difficult, but it is not, I think, impossible. It is to diffuse throughout the college, its graduates and friends, its governing board, its faculty, its students, its athletic management and coaching staff—it is to diffuse, I say, throughout the institution a vigilant integrity—a conscience which will be active and on the alert to make sure that any football team or any other team which represents the college in any intercollegiate sport is really representative of the college, that it is built up out of a student body which has been attracted to the college by its character, its quality, and its reputation as an institution of learning; that it is bone of its bone and flesh of its flesh, and not something extraneous to the college; not something which has been brought into a quasi relationship to it by emoluments, inducements, or persuasions which have nothing whatever to do with the drawing power of the college itself; in a word, something which is not foreign, but out own.

This honest way means, moreover, that athletics are made part and parcel of the educational process, both in respect to the athlete himself and to the student body as a whole.

Again, as to the student body in general—those who play the game from the grandstand. I have always felt that in our educational procedure we take too little account of the emotions and make too little appeal to them, and I think there is a clear value in the pageant of enthusiasm which is staged around an intercollegiate game. Our hearts are quickened by the flag; we are carried out of ourselves into a unity of spirit; we feel as one man the "glory" of Colorado and we "hurrah for the Silver and the Gold." This seems to me to be a good thing to do. The highest of the emotions is loyalty to something outside of ourselves and we do well to give expression to it now and again. But if we are to "holler our heads off" on such occasions, then it seems rather important that we should have something to "holler" about; in other words, if that pageant of enthusiasm is not to be a crude surrender to imbecile frenzy, then it seems to me rather important that it be staged about something which is our own, something which has been enlisted out of our own life, and not something which is imported from abroad. Mercenary armies have at times imspired men's fears and hopes, but they have never evoked a people's patriotism.

When Norlin became president of the university, the traditional role of the humanities in the curricula of American colleges and universities was being challenged by the expanding importance of the sciences and the social sciences, and by the new professional schools organized to meet the needs of American industry for technical knowledge. Many scholars, too, were shifting from the study of the classic knowledge of the past to hands-on research in laboratories.

The state universities in the Midwest and the West were gaining in enrollments and influence. Unlike the earlier private colleges and universities in the East, the educational policies of these public institutions were decided, indirectly, by the state legislatures through their power of the purse. In Colorado, as in most states, the legislators knew little or nothing about the complex purposes of their university nor, consequently, how the money they appropriated to support it would be used.

With the convening of each annual legislative session, therefore, Norlin had to begin anew to educate the Colorado senators and representatives, then persuade them to provide adequate funds for the university—often in the face of powerful political forces. In 1924, for example, the Colorado legislature was controlled by members of the Ku Klux Klan. Governor Clarence J. Morley, elected with considerable help from the Klan, demanded that Norlin dismiss all Jews and Catholics on the faculty or he would cut off the university's appropriation from the legislature. Norlin promptly refused. Shortly thereafter, fortunately, the governor backed down.

Norlin also devoted much time and energy educating ordinary citizens—and taxpayers—of Colorado about the purposes of their university, primarily through speeches to civic organizations and other groups of concerned citizens. The speeches that follow are typical.

Professor of Greek

THE ROLE OF HIGHER EDUCATION IN A FRONTIER DEMOCRATIC SOCIETY

1. The Purpose of a University

What then, is the purpose which the true university always fights to keep uppermost? Let me try to answer that by recalling to you a relay race in ancient Athens—a race run by night, in which each runner carried a torch to the runner ahead. If the runners ran too slow, they lost the race. If they ran too fast and extinguished the torch, they defeated themselves. The object was to carry the torch with due speed, but undimmed, to the goal. And that in a figure, is the object of the university.

The point that I wish to make in what I have been saying is that is all of us in the university, faculty and students, will lay to heart the purpose of the university and never cease to cherish it, then we need not to be too much concerned about the machinery and machinations of academic routine. These are trappings that come and go, and none of us needs to be their slave unless we choose to mistake them for the university itself. Nor need we be too much concerned about overemphasis on wholesome associations of university life, such as social recreation and athletics, unless we choose to mistake them for the university itself. There is, for example, no occasion to become overexcited when a collegiate fraternity attempts to exalt its local standing by recruiting a battery of athletes from a neighboring state;

that sort of blindness cannot long survive where there is a proper vision of a university.

"Where there is no vision, the people perish," says our sacred book. Where there is no vision the university perishes, in fact if not in name. It is the spirit that giveth life. And as I stand here this morning full of hope and faith in you who now constitute the University of Colorado, I can wish no better thing than that we may be possessed now and throughout the year by that university spirit which alone can give zest and meaning and fruitfulness and joy to our living together both in our work and in our play.

2. *The Role of a State University*

Some one said to me the other day, "Why are you so much concerned about the university? You are soon to retire, and the fortune of the university does not affect you personally," to which my reply was that I was like the cowboy who grabbed a Texas steer by the tail, thinking that he could control him, only to find himself bounced over the prairie through cactus and thorn bushes until he lost his clothes and some of his skin. When some one yelled at him, "You fool, why don't you let go?" "Let go?" he said, "it's all I can do to hang on."

Well, the fact that though I am hanging on I shall soon let go may enable me to speak of the university more objectively and less personally that if I were continuing in my present office for an indefinite period.

I shall not discuss here the mooted question of what fields of education and training the unviersity should cover, except to say that the fundamental purpose of a university is to bring each generation into step with the forward strides of the race through its courses in the college of liberal arts and those of its professional schools as well. John Bright once said in an eloquent speech, "We stand on the shoulders of our ancestors and we can see farther than they." That is only a half-truth, which many applaud. The other half of the truth is that we must climb up to the shoulders of our ancestors in order to be able to see farther than they. It is the fundamental business of the university to enable us to climb to the topmost levels reached by civilization, and from that vantage ground to see farther and to go farther.

This sort of education is one which should be placed within reach of all who are capable of profiting by it, whether rich or poor. The state university is the instrument which is devised to do this very thing. The purpose of its founders was to equalize educational opportunity in higher education, and most state universities have started on the basis of making no tuition charges. Most of them have departed from this idea in more or less degree. I regret that the University of Colorado has been compelled to depart from it more than the others. In fact the University of Colorado is almost unique among state universities in the fact that student tuition and fees now constitute almost half of the revenue for operating expenses. This is not as it should be. Many worthy and competent students are barred from the university because they cannot afford to pay the cost.

It is a commonplace to say that a university, and particularly a state university, exists for the propagation of truth, not of half-truths, not of truth colored or distorted by selfish interests, and not of half-baked ideas. How important this is especially in a democratic society is not fully realized. Few people appreciate the extent to which our ideas and attitudes of mind are colored or formed or fixed by agencies and influences that are commercial in this character—agencies whose primary motive is not the dissemination of truth but the making of money. The school, the university seek their dividends alone in the intelligence and character of those whom they serve.

It is, therefore, vitally important that the scholar, the teacher should be free to speak the truth, each as he sees it. Every pain should be taken to see to it that he is a scholar in the sense that he knows whereof he speaks. There is no place in a university for agitators or propagandists or soapbox orators, but there is a place for any man who is capable of shedding the sort of light which dispels the darkness of cant and superstition and prejudice and ignorance. He that is a scholar and a teacher in that sense must be free, and secure in his freedom. There must be security of tenure so that he may not be afraid of losing his job if he runs counter to the prejudice which it is his business to break down.

Also the university as an institution should have some sense of security. It should be enabled to stand up in a storm. A state university should be the deliberate expression of the will of the people of the state. But that is not to say that it should bend to every momentary wind that blows. Even a legislature has been known to be carried away by ideas which have the impermanence of a whirlwind. Therefore, it is highly important that a state university should have a stable source of income apart from short-term appropriations about which there is always uncertainty.

There is a general movement throughout the country to centralize the control over state educational institutions in the state capitol building. That is, I think, very dangerous. That means political control and the death of freedom in our state institutions of higher learning. If democracy is to be more than a hollow mockery, let the schools and universities be free!

It should be, I think, the other way around. The state

educational institutions should have more influence than they now do upon the political and social life of our state. The state university should not be confined to the campus. It should not be a partisan in political conflicts, but it should be a center of dissemination of facts and truth among the people of the state regarding questions on which they desire disinterested information.

It is this function of a state university which is much challenged. If the university through competent members of the faculty makes and publishes impartial studies of the facts with regard to problems that confront the people of the state, we arouse the ire of some faction of the state and are told to "mind our own business." Even some of our friends take the view that the university should establish itself in the good will of the people of the state by offending nobody.

But what is the university's business? My view is that it is the university's business to disseminate truth wherever the truth is serviceable and needed. If the people of the state really want to exclude the university from those things which agitate their minds from time to time, it is for them to say. This is their university. I only know that the university is capable of doing an immensely greater service to our people if they want it to do so and are willing to give it the means of doing so.

3. The Value of Traditional Subjects

We have not outgrown the teachings of Socrates and Plato. We have not outgrown the Sermon on the Mount. There are a thousand voices calling to us from the past, here warning us and restraining us, there pointing us onward, reviving us when we are spent, and ever kindling afresh the divine flame. We cannot afford to stop our ears to them. There are a thousand battlefields of the past where men have fought and died that we may have life and have it more abundantly. We cannot afford to be ignorant of them. There are a thousand noble spirits who have dragged themselves from the mud, climbed the heights, and caught the larger view. We cannot afford to forego their companionship. "Is not life more than meat and the body more than raiment?" It is the first business of the home, of the church, and, above all, of the school, to keep civilization alive. Whatever else formal education should take into account, it is, I insist, its first business to see to it that, as far as possible, every individual shall embody in his life, his experience, his sympathies, his character—the forward strides of the race. This is a large order, and I do not mean to contend that from this point of view our high-school curricula are ideal. There are sins of omission and commission, but in the main the so-called traditional subjects have their values and their justification in the fact that they are gateways to a knowledge of the greatest and highest accomplishments of mankind. But, you may say, they are only gateways which many never step through. There may, indeed, be something amusing even in the suggestion that the pathetic groping of the pupil through declensions and conjugations is a groping for the light, but it is no more amusing and no more absurd than that the inarticulate lispings of the child could ever have been formed into the splendid utterances of the Pslams or the unrivalled eloquence of Shakespeare. If we can make a right approach it is something. Whether we can do more depends entirely on our training and power; whether the subjects we teach seem dead because they deal with a past that seems dead. The past is not dead. It lives on in our speech, our habits, our thoughts, our institutions. There are, for example, no dead languages, no dead literatures, in our curricula. Latin and Greek live on—

and if we who are teachers do not look before and after, do not relate the present to the past and the past to the present, it is we who are dead, not they.

4. Liberal Scholars As Teachers

It requires above all that we restore to the college the type of liberal scholar and teacher whose passing from the academic world has been lamented by us all. Here lies our great difficulty. But we are not without responsibility for his going, and I dare say that in time we can recall him if only we are prepared to give to him—what we have denied to him in the past quarter century—his due place and his due reward in the college; especially if we can persuade our graduate schools to recognize that not the least important part of their great function is to train scholars who, plucking the flower out of the crannies, will attempt to see in it and make others see in it what God and man is—scholars, I mean, who can teach. After all, it is a question of men. The right sort of men will interest our undergraduates in the intellectual life in spite of all our machinations and our methods. Most of us, fortunately, have even now such men on our faculties, and we thank God for them as we see what they can do with students.

5. The Value Of The Classics

I read and reread as a bracing tonic Plato's report of Socrates' defense before the red-hunting jury which condemned him to death for his subversive teaching. It is one of the two great testaments of all time. It grows upon me more and more year by year. Socrates is as much alive to me as he was before he drank the hemlock which slowly stole away that sweet, brave life. He is as real to me as any one of you—more real, perhaps, for I know him better—and I cannot imagine how I could do without his companionship. Even now I hear his firm but uncomplaining words spoke in the face of death, refusing to compromise with truth, refusing to buy his life at the price of not teaching any more.

"Men of Athens, I hold you in honor and affection, but I will obey God rather than you; and as long as I have the breath of life and the strength to do so I shall never cease my pursuit of truth, I shall never cease exhorting whomsoever of you I meet and challenging him and saying in my usual way: 'My friend, you who belong to that city which is the greatest and the most renowned for wisdom and power, are you not ashamed that your heart is set on heaping up wealth and reputation and honor, while for the amassing of intelligence and truth and the soul's highest goods, you do not care nor give it a thought? 'For I do nothing but go about trying to persuade you all, old and young alike, not to take first thought for your bodies or for your worldly goods, but to put first and foremost the improvement of your souls, verily saying to you that virtue is not purchasable by money, but that, on the contrary, from virtue stems prosperity and all the other good things which come to men whether in private or public life. If by these doctrines I am corrupting our youth, then so much the worse for these doctrines. But if any one says that I speak other words than these, he says what is not so.

"Wherefore, men of Athens, I would say to you, believe my accuser or not as you please, acquit me or not as you please, but no matter what you do, I shall not change my course even if I were to die over and over again."

These are bracing words, and he who does not feel in

his own heart the tonic of them and of other words like them is cheated of his heritage.

6. "Whom, Then, Do I Call Educated?"

"Whom, then, do I call educated?" Socrates asks. "First, those who manage well the circumstances which they encounter day by day, and who possess a judgment which is accurate in meeting occasions as they rise and rarely miss the expedient course of action; next, those who are decent and honorable in their intercourse with all men, bearing easily and good-naturedly what is unpleasant or offensive in others, and being themselves as agreeable and reasonable to their associates as it is humanly possible to be; furthermore, those who hold their pleasures always under control and are not unduly overcome by their misfortunes, bearing up under them bravely and in a manner worthy of our common nature; finally, and most important of all, those who are not spoiled by their successes and do not desert their true selves, but hold their ground steadfastly as wise and sober-minded men, rejoicing no more in the good things which have come to them through chance than in those which through their own nature and intelligence are theirs from birth. Those who have a character which is in accord, not with one of these things, but with all of them—these I maintain are educated and whole men, possessed of all the virtues of man."

·III·

NAZISM, FASCISM, NATIONALISM, ISOLATIONISM AND THE COMING OF WORLD WAR II

In 1931 Norlin accepted an invitation to teach at the University of Berlin as the Theordore Roosevelt Professor of American Life and Institutions. He and Mrs. Norlin spent the academic year of 1932–1933 in Germany, staying at the same hotel in which Adolf Hitler resided. The führer, in Norlin's terse opinion, "was not a man you would go fishing with."

The Norlins' many unpleasant encounters with the "dreadful Nazis"—Jew-baiting by the Nazi students, burning of books, rampant injustice and persecution, blatant lies, unwarranted arrogance—all made vivid impressions on their minds. Norlin became convinced that if Nazism was allowed to thrive and spread it would endanger democratic values everywhere.

But when the Norlins returned to the United States in the summer of 1933, they found few Americans shared their convictions. Apathy was the dominant mood of the country. "America First" was not only a popular slogan, it was also a powerful political force. Still, Norlin had such a "passionate faith in democracy" he simply could not remain silent, even in the face of such overwhelming indifference. He wrote articles for national magazines and newspapers, delivered speeches throughout the country, all "pleading that the human quality of militancy . . . be quickened out of its deathly stupor in civilized countries and marshalled vigilantly in defense of the humanity which lifts us above brute creation."

It was an unpopular cause, and Norlin had only modest success. He was a man with a message ahead of his time. And it wasn't until the Japanese attacked Pearl Harbor that Americans were roused, overnight, from their years of indifference to events beyond their shores.

Of his many published articles and speeches on Hitler and the rise of nationalism, I've selected three that best represent the ideas Norlin was trying to get across to the American people.

THOUGHTS OF ONE IN SOLITARY CONFINEMENT: PRIVATE

Today while three doctors were putting their heads together in my sick room over a matter which was not very serious, I remarked with one of those little satisfactions which one can still squeeze out of a troubled existence, "Good for the Czechoslovakian Legionnaires. They have returned to the King of England and to the French Republic the citations and decorations which the members of that Legion had received from them whilst fighting in the Great War to preserve England and France from conquest and devastation—an interesting situation. Honor and glory are now for those who conquer and devastate."

I supposed that thoughts like these were uppermost (this was Sunday) in the minds of the doctors too and that they must have felt for a day at least that their professional tasks were relatively perfunctory and unimportant. But my remark provoked no response whatsoever except a furtive exchange of glances on their part, which said almost in so many words, "We have here a delirious condition."

This startled me a bit at first. Then I began to wonder. Were they perhaps right? They seemed normal and healthy and to be about their business with gusto. For a day or so they had read the headlines with unusual curiosity. Things had looked rather unsettled. But the good old world had righted itself once more and happier days were here again on the stock exchange.

Also the world in general felt the same way. Prayers that peace—peace at any sacrifice—might come out of

Returning from his lectureship at the University of Berlin, 1933

the Munich conference had been answered. Te deums were sung with extraordinary fervor in the cathedrals, bells were pealing, men were shouting—all the world was glad. Was I suffering from a mind diseased? Was it not a symptom of madness in me that all the world seemed mad? Was I, indeed, mad?

Quite honestly, I do not feel competent to answer. I will leave the question open. Events will answer it. Only (and this may be part of my madness) I have little or no hope that events will justify our present feeling of security and joy.

The one thing that I cannot understand, assuming that the world in general is sane, is that the butchering of Czechoslovakia by the Munich conference was received outside of Germany and Italy (as in Germany and Italy) as a great accomplishment—a triumph of humanity. Every nation represented at Munich and also our own United States are claiming credit for the glory of that accomplishment. And I suppose that henceforth the great prize of the souvenir hunters will be a splinter of Czechoslovakia, whose wreck saved the world.

Now I am willing to admit sincerely the possibility that as things now are, *any peace is better than any war* and that freedom and honor and truth and justice may be mere abstractions to be brushed aside when we are face to face with the utter extermination of all but the baser instincts of men, which a European or world war might bring about. And if I admit this possibility, then I should go further, perhaps, and admit the possibility that Chamberlain and Daladier were sensible (though not demigods) in yielding to every essential demand of Hitler and Mussolini and in forcing the dismemberment and ultimate destruction of the only surviving democracy in central Europe.

But admitting these possibilities, I am utterly amazed

at the hypocrisy with which the events of the past week have been interpreted. It is the most striking and the most shameless example of rationalizing which I have seen outside of Germany and Italy in many years.

The talk is as if there was on Saturday a great choice between good and evil, and that the good was chosen.

But the choice was not between good and evil, but at best between an instant war (I do not think it was instant) and the scrapping of treaties and honor among nations. And the most that our wishful thinking may make out of it is that the lesser evil was arrived at.

If the conference be regarded as *successful*, the success lay simply in this: England and France by lying down supinely before Hitler and Mussolini and by threatening Czechoslovakia with force; by strengthening immeasurably and virtually aligning themselves with the arrogant bullies of European politics won a moment's respite from the war, which may be the more terrible because of that respite, unless there comes about soon a complete change of heart in the aggressor nations, of which there is not the slightest indication.

No principle of international ethics was urged seriously in the Munich conference. The plea of self-determination was so false and mawkish that all the horses in the world burst into laughter.

But out of the conference, which had nothing to do with upholding principles, which was not indeed a conference at all but a meeting of dictators, there emerged an idea, a principle, which though not clothed in words, stood out with unmistakable meaning and sinister colors before all the world—the idea that a nation sins against the world by being small, that it is guilty of the naivest folly in relying on strong friends in foul weather, and that its best course—its most ethical course—is to win security and peace by yielding to the conquest of superior powers. We have been familiar with that idea in Italy and Germany and Japan. Now it has been sanctioned by the United Kingdom, by France, and by the United States—by all the great democracies. (The little powers, of course, don't count.)

This is a consummation which may be sensible, but it is one not devoutly to be wished. At best it should be acquiesced in the faces covered and heads bowed in humiliation—with fasting and prayer—and with the wistful hope that out of a shameful truce may come somehow an honorable peace, and that life may reverse its laws so that out of something which we know to be evil good may come.

The monstrous pretense that the "Peace of Munich" is a triumph of the forces of civilization is the most ominous thing in the whole situation. We are fooling ourselves terribly and progressively. Even now we do not know the difference between good and evil. There is some hope for us and some health in us as long as we are able to call things by their right names, but Plato's "lie in the soul" is a deathly canker.

OUR NATIONAL DEFENSES

In addressing you at this Honors Convocation I am breaking three precedents. First, I attempt, though by request, to fill the shoes of a celebrity from abroad. Second, I violate the proprieties of what is supposed to be an academic occasion, sheltered and aloof from the storms which rage over the world, on which the lecturer at least should be characterized by an unruffled, Olympian calm.

"It is sweet," said the ancient philosopher, Lucretius, "to look upon the mighty contests of war arrayed along the plains without yourself sharing in the danger; it is sweet to hold the lofty and serene positions well fortified by the learning of the wise from which you may look down upon others and see them wandering all about and going astray in their search for the path of life . . . their striving night and day with surpassing effort to struggle up to the summit of power and be masters of the world."

I confess at once my inability to rise to such philosophical aloofness at a time when the very citadels of learning and wisdom are the least secure from the wild forces which seek to master the world.

Third, I neglect the fundamental precept to the orator that he should align himself, or appear to align himself, with the sentiments, even the prejudices, of his hearers. According to a recent poll of the Institute of Public Opinion, seventy per cent of my fellow countrymen are against what I feel and think and what I shall try to say this afternoon.

Now I am not one of those who think that the minority is always right and the majority always wrong. In fact I believe that by and large and in the long run the majority is most apt to be right, and I feel on the defensive for not being of it. Am I right or wrong? Let me be quite honest and say I do not pretend to know for sure.

But one thing I do know and am sure of and that is that we are all terribly tempted when we are perplexed and perturbed in mind and heart to seek refuge from ourselves in the crowd. There is a great comfort in the escape from personal isolation into a oneness with others, into a keeping of step with a regiment, into a spiritual regimentation.

Anarchy is revolting to our nature. We have an instinct for order, and when we feel unequal to setting our own house in order, we long for some one to order us about, for someone to be the captain of our souls. And when he comes, we acclaim him gladly. Heil Hitler, viva Mussolini. That is one main reason why there is such a passion for regimentation in the world today. Men are tired of the anarchy in their own souls, and in order to escape from this personal thralldom they are quite willing to lose themselves in the mob and to put on other chains.

That is, I say, a dangerous temptation, which more than any other must be resisted by each and every one of us every day and every hour if we care to live under a democracy and to preserve the democratic way of life. Let this be a warning to you against going with the crowd and at the same time a caution to you not to accept the views which I shall express without examination on your part. You must do what is the most difficult thing in the world to do, namely, set your own house in order.

I appreciate that I am speaking to you partly out of an experience which most of you have not shared, and happily cannot share, though you do, unhappily, share in its consequence. The horrors of the World War and its more terrible aftermath of the devastations which it wrought in the souls of men are to me a present nightmare from which I struggle to awake and cannot. I would not bring that experience home to you if I could, and I could not if I would. To you it is an episode in history. You know of it at second hand, from hearsay.

I could wish that that hearsay were more in accord with truth. Certainly it is not in accord with the whole truth. For there has grown up in our country what I call a national myth. I do not know just why or how except that a prolonged debauch of dreams and emotions such as we give ourselves over to during that war is inevitably followed by a depressing morning after—a period of disillusionment when it is only human to seek some scapegoat for the blasting of our hopes. At any rate there is a general attitude of mind to the effect that we were fooled into participation in the World War, that we were pushed into it by bankers and big business and by foreign propaganda and that we are never, never going to be fooled again.

Well, let us never be fooled again, and let us not be fooled now. In fact we pushed ourselves into that war. And why? Because we felt that isolation from that conflict was unworthy of us; because we felt that the issue of that conflict was of profound concern to us; because we felt deeply that though in some respects the motives and aims of the combatants were mixed and confused, yet we had precious and vital interests in common with one side against the other; because we had been moved to indignation by the brutal treaty; because we were more sensitive than we are now to the sinking of American ships by a foreign power; and, above all, because we were lifted up on the wings of a high hope—the great hope that if we threw into that war our power, our prestige, and our relative detachment from the quarrels of Europe we would be in a strong position to see to it that out of the ashes of that conflict there would grow some parliament of man, some world league, which could prevent such cataclysms in the future. It was, we thought, a war to end all war.

Well, it did not turn out so. We were on the side of the victors, but we won nothing for which we fought. Why? Because of Clemenceau? Because of Lloyd George? Because Woodrow Wilson was a schoolmaster unable to cope with Machiavellians? Or was it that we were unable to follow up our victory and reap its fruits because a minority in the Senate of the United States, hating the president and his initiative, made it impossible for us to join with other nations in a league for peace?

In fact, we fought and won and ran away. We left the League of Nations, the child begotten of American aspirations, a foundling upon the doorstep of Europe; we crawled into our own skins and condemned the nations across the Atlantic, outworn, impoverished, their wounds still raw and bleeding, their hearts torn by rancor and hate, to "stew in their own juice"; and so we made the world safe, not for democracy, but for gangsterism.

It is a marvel that the League of Nations, disowned by us, has lived as long as it has, without our support. Its membership has never given up the hope that we would somehow work with them, whether as members of the league or outside the league, in a collective effort to preserve civilization. And in that hope the league has kept alive, and in the dashing of that hope it has become for a time a ghost to haunt our dreams.

Had we been willing to join with the nations of the

league in putting an embargo upon exports without which Italy would have been helpless, we could have prevented the conquest of Ethiopia. The Italian invasion was a motor power invasion. Italy had no oil. But what did we do? We actually contributed to the joy ride of Mussolini by sending him trucks and oil and gasoline in plenty. In effect, we helped in the devastation of Ethiopia. Mussolini himself said as much in his speech to his Cabinet on March 3, 1936, when he expressed his gratitude to the United States for our noncooperation with the League of Nations.

Again, we "hamstrung" the power of the league in its attempt to prevent the rape of China by Japan. Read, if you will, Mr. Henry L. Stimson's thoughtful book, *The Crisis in the Orient.* (Mr. Stimson, you remember, was the very able secretary of state in the Hoover administration.) Or read his more recent letter, published in the *New York Times* of the sixth of last November. He points out that the United States and Great Britain are furnishing most of the sinews of war to Japan, that cooperation between these two countries alone in withholding supplies would shortly bring Japan to a standstill, and that by refusing such cooperation, we of the United States, while sympathizing with China, are really aiding and abetting Japan. "China's principal need," he says, "is not that something should be done by outside nations to help her but that outside nations should cease helping her enemy."

Mr. Stimson then asks this question: "Is the condition of our statemanship so pitifully inadequate that we cannot devise the simple means of international cooperation which would stop our participation in their slaughter?"

These words of Mr. Stimson are not applicable to the present able secretary of state nor the president of the

United States. Even when Mr. Stimson was writing the letter from which I have quoted, President Roosevelt, in his speech at Chicago on October 5, looking not only to Japan but to the other great powers, Italy and Germany, which have made war and violence the foundation of their foreign policy, said in effect in strong and emphatic terms that the people of the United States, no less than the other peoples, were in great danger of being engulfed in a chaos of violence and brutality and that our safety lay, not in aloofness, not in isolation, not in neutrality, but in active and positive cooperation with other peace-loving countries.

That speech seemed to indicate a sharp departure from our policy of going it alone all these years. In the language of President Butler of Columbia University, "it quickened and heartened the spirit of the whole world." It recalled another occasion when the words of another president of the United States twenty years ago in like manner and matter "quickened and heartened the spirit of the whole world." And last October and November the League of Nations turned with fresh hope to the United States.

But the president of the United States in 1937, like the president of the United States in 1919, had spoken from his heart, without reckoning with Congress. For following the president's Chicago speech Congress was deluged with telegrams and letters against any form of international cooperation. The isolationists made a tremendous noise. They almost passed the Ludlow Amendment. Mr. Hull of the Department of State was forced into a public declaration that the policy of the United States was to travel its own road. No company wanted.

Then came the shattering news from abroad. The prime minister of Great Britain had scuttled the League of Nations, dismissed Mr. Eden from the Foreign Office, and set out to make terms with the barbarism of Hitler and Mussolini.

Of course we were and are disappointed in the English government. It is one thing for us to isolate ourselves from the English, and quite another thing for the English to isolate themselves from us. It is one thing to isolate ourselves and quite another thing to have isolation thrust upon us.

Well, we are reaping the fruits of our isolation, and they are not sweet, but bitter and poisonous. International cooperation—a solid front—seems for the moment out of the question, but only for the moment.

Great Britain will discover, if it has not already been brought home to her by the forcible annexation of Austria by a power which one day guaranteed the independence of Austria and a few days after marched in triumph into her capital, that no terms can be made with those who make and break treaties without conscience and without honor, and that capitulation to the sworn enemies of democracy means the death of democracy in Europe. And we of the United States will discover (let us hope not too late) that unless we can help actively and positively to turn the course of history in the right direction, for our democracy, too, the pallbearers stand ready at the door.

Our fear of foreign entanglements, even of association with foreigners, seems to me a curious thing. We are afraid that foreign diplomats are too "slick" for us: that they will use us to "pull their chestnuts out of the fire." But that argues an incredible degree of stupidity on our part. If we are as stupid as that, can we be trusted to pull our own chestnuts out of the fire?

But for the moment what? Mr. Hoover, home from European travels and a visit with Hitler, made an eloquent speech the other day, telling us what our course should be. That speech deserves attention because his opinions are entitled to respect and are, furthermore, I believe, the opinions of the majority of our people.

The keynote of that speech, as reported in the press, is "mind our own business." He warns us specifically against joining a democratic front with Britain and France. "We should have none of it," he said; "if the world is to keep the peace then we must keep the peace with dictatorships as well as with popular governments. The form of government which other peoples pass through in working out their destinies is not our business."

But let us pause for a moment and examine into this declaration of policy. (It is, by the way, exactly the policy which we have blamed the Chamberlain government in London for embarking upon.) If Mr. Hoover means by a democratic front a military alliance with Britain and France to promote democracy where it is not wanted, that is one thing. But if he means that we should not stand by Britain and France in preserving democracy where it is wanted, in checking a Fascist internazionale from forcing itsef upon unwilling countries, that is quite another thing. (I leave the Communist dictatorship out of this discussion, because Russia is not now a threat to world peace, but the contrary.) Does Mr. Hoover really think that the Spaniards or the Austrians are working out their own destinies, or that even the peoples of Germany and Italy and Japan are working out their own destinies?

We have no quarrel with the domestic policy of a free people. But when the whole policy and philosophy of a ruling power is to weld the people of the nation by terrorism and propaganda into a monstrous engine of destruction and to glorify war and conquest as the supreme function of the state, when, in other words, the internal policy of the state is built into a foreign policy of ruthless aggression, that is a matter of grave concern to all who want to go about their business in freedom and in peace. Mr. Hoover admits (I quote his own words) that "Fascism is already a raging power, which no longer holds to its original boundaries, but has spread to fourteen European nations with two hundred and forty million people."

What is our own business? A few years ago some sixty nations under the Pact of Paris, better known as the Kellogg Peace Pact, entered into solemn convenants with us to renounce war as an instrument of national policy. Is it none of our business that signatories to that treaty with us have renounced, not war, but the renunciation of war? Again, some years ago we initiated at Washington the Nine-Power Treaty, under which nine world powers, including ourselves and Japan, pledged themselves to respect the integrity and independence of China. What does that mean? In our constitution there is a clause which provides that "treaties made, or which shall be made, under the authority of the United States, shall be the supreme law of the land." Are we, then, faithful to the supreme law of our land in keeping peace and friendly diplomatic relations with a signatory to that treaty which is overrunning China with fire and sword? Are treaties which we sign the supreme law of our land? Or are they for us, too, scraps of paper?

What is our business? If there should break out tomorrow a war between Germany and Czechoslovakia, should we do what we have done in the case of Italy and Japan—furnish the raw materials of war to aid German aggression as we would do under the operation of our miscalled Neutrality Act? Our neutrality law is our "mind our own business" law; it is what I call our dugout law. But in effect it aligns us with the strong against the weak, with a country which has a navy and a merchant marine against one which is lacking in these advantages, with aggressor nations against those who want to go their own way in peace. Is that minding our own business?

Mr. Hoover is opposed to our having anything to do with collective action. He does, however, urge upon us our duty to join in the force of collective sentiment. If this did not come from an able ex-president of the United States it might sound naive. We have expressed ourselves morally in company with other nations. We have again and again joined with them in moral astringents. Only last November at the Brussel's conference we joined in saying to Japan in effect, "What you are doing isn't cricket. Won't you please play the game according to the rules?" The answer was the wholesale bombing of Chinese noncombatants—helpless men, women, and children.

Such moral protests have been as deterrent to the warmongers as squeal of a rabbit to a wolf. I am reminded of a speech by John Bright in the House of Commons in which he told of a man who set out to make a fortune by manufacturing pills for the cure of earthquakes.

Mr. Hoover does couple moral force with military preparedness. Preparedness for what? Does he mean that we should put teeth in our moral suasion by threat or use of physical force? Does he mean that we should enforce treaties and international morals by force of arms?

He doesn't mean that. What does he mean? Is he as confused about this as Congress now seems to be, as the mild and pacific Senator Norris seems to be, favoring a large navy without quite knowing what it is to be used for?

Senator Norris was one of the eight senators who voted against our going into the World War. He was then an extreme pacifist. Now he has modified his views. "I feel bound," he said the other day, "to keep our country armed to an extent greater than Japan is armed or greater than either Italy or Germany is armed." "Since," he adds, "it seems almost as if these nations have gone wild and lost all sense of decency and honor."

We must, he thinks, be prepared to meet this wildness somehow, though he does not see why we should indulge in quite so wild a navy spree.

In that point of view many of us agree. But where are we to meet this wildness, and when? President Roosevelt in arguing for a mammoth navy has explained that we must defend ourselves by meeting the enemy, not on or at our borders, but long before they reach our shores. Where, then, is the line of our defense?

Except for our distant outposts, like the Philippines, which our isolationists seem quite ready to throw to the wolves, military invasion of our soil seems as yet a remote possibility. There is, however, danger of another sort which is not remote. In one sense the enemy has already crashed our gates and is advancing steadily upon us. President Roosevelt in his forthright Chicago speech called down upon himself the wrath of all who would save their own skins by crawling into their own skins when he used the wicked word "quarantine." Yet it was an appropriate word. He was expressing himself as an isolationist of a different kind. He was speaking of the necessity of an international concert to isolate the madness of fascism and prevent its further spread, not only in the material sense but in the realm of the spirit.

As things are now, or rather, as things are going, there is no quarantine against ideas which are the more contagious the more they are diseased. They are not stopped by fortifications; they mock at armies and navies;

they overleap the barriers of oceans; and they take possession of any soil where, to use a medical term, there are no antibodies to resist them.

Our spiritual defenses are down. We are divided among ourselves as a nation. There seems to be no clear-cut vigorous national philosophy or faith to bind us together into a spiritual union. In our disunion we cannot but envy the solidarity of fascism, its driving power, its spectacular successes, and without strong convictions of our own we permit its fanaticisms to land on our soil, to invade our homes, and to work havoc in our souls.

One of our own students, a graduate of our medical school, a fine boy with brilliant promise, was invited not long ago to join the staff of an American hospital. When he reported for duty he was told regretfully that Fascist prejudice in the governing board refused to approve his appointment.

Does anyone suppose that there is no relation between the accentuation of anti-Semitism in this country and the fire which is consuming the Jews in Europe?

Does anyone suppose that there is no relation between the spread of crime and the lowering of morals in this country and the fact that whole nations have trampled morals under foot and proclaimed it to be divinely righteous for the state to lie, to steal, and to murder whenever crime seems to advantage the state?

Does anyone suppose that there is no relation between the growing cheapening of human life among us—the dulling of the edge of our concern for human beings—and the wholesale slaughter of innocents, yesterday in Ethiopia, today in China and Spain, tomorrow God knows where?

Does anyone suppose that there is no relation between the triumphal march of Nazi brutality in central Europe and the sentiment which one hears on the streets of Boulder or of Denver or of any American town, that "what this country needs is a Hitler?"

That colossal barbarism is debauching us all. There is little danger that you and I may be exiled from our country as others like us have been exiled from Germany or Italy or Austria, but there is danger that we may be exiled from the way of life which many of us regard as more precious than life itself. It is not at all inconceivable that if and when we shall have built up the biggest and the strongest armaments on earth, we shall have lost our souls to the enemy and there will be nothing left worth fighting for.

These words may sound like those of an alarmist, and perhaps they are. Forget them if you want to, but I would not have you forget what I now say.

This planet is now a great battleground in which two ideas or two sets of ideas—two philosophies—are struggling for supremacy. Not that they face each other for the first time. They have met before on a thousand battlefields—nations against nations, parties against parties, blocs against blocs, man against man, individuals against themselves. But they are now met in a colossal struggle such as the world has never before seen, and the issue of the conflict seems to be in some final sense fateful for mankind.

Two ideas, two sets of ideas, two philosophies—what are they? The one philosophy regards human beings as means to an end, as material for exploitation, though it has seldom been nakedly frank in doing so. Almost always it wears the guise of benevolence. For example, the institution of human slavery not so long ago was preached as a divine ordinance—good for master, good for man. And I have no doubt that the rules of ancient Egypt thought it good for their subjects to be lashed into the building of pyramids.

Fascism, too, grins beneath a mask of patriotism, but fascism is in reality the exploitation of human beings on a national scale. It has no regard whatsoever for human life as such, not even the life of its own subjects. They have no rights, not even the right to live. They are of value only as they contribute to the power of the state. They are just so many cells in a vast organism. If they do not function, or are suspected not to function, healthily and loyally, they are cancerous growths which must be removed by ruthless surgery. They are to all intents and purposes slaves, whipped into step by a leader alias a driver. The only freedom is the freedom of the state to work its absolute will, and the will of the Fascist state is war. All the domestic regimentation of the people is for one end—the complete militarization of the state, the welding of every man, woman, and child of the nation into a unified, smooth-running, invincible machine of destruction—a machine which is beyond good and evil, which is a law unto itself, which is unmoral and elemental, having no more conscience than an earthquake or a flood. It is, in fact, more cruel than nature in her most savage moods. For nature is merely indifferent to our human kind, whereas this monstrous violence seeks out men, women, and children for destruction. Fascism strives for the triumph of death over life.

These are strong words. One can hardly credit that they are true. It seems beyond belief that such a philosophy even when implemented by a terrorism which is without parallel in its ruthlessness and by a propaganda more thoroughgoing than any which has ever tried to shape or distort the souls of men—it seems, I say, beyond belief that such a philosophy could be rammed down the throats of millions upon millions of supposedly rational beings. Yet it is not altogether incredible to one who has witnessed the triumph of fascism or nazism on the ground.

It is not the whole story to say that fascism has been foisted upon unwilling people. It has, in fact, been welcomed by many people. It has appealed to all whose love of country was measured by hatred of other peoples; it has appealed to the privileged classes, who expected to use the new regime to their own ends; it has appealed to the hungry and destitute, who found in it promise of bread; it has appealed to the down-and-outers, who hoped the revolution would give them a place in the sun; it has appealed to the nobodies who, strutting in uniforms, became swollen with a sense of their own importance; it has appealed to the brutally minded, who under the restraints of civilization had never before been free to express themselves adequately, and to the criminally minded, who now found their lawless instincts sublimated by patriotism; and it has appealed to a large mixed group of the middle-aged and the young, especially the young, who, distraught by the mental and moral disintegration of their lives, and oppressed by a sense of the aloneness and futility of their individual existence, gladly lost themselves in the crowd, merged themselves with the mob, and joined the march towards the dazzling glory of imperial power.

Fascism is, therefore, in a sense, the religion of lost souls, and there is point to the observation of Heywood Broun that those who have lost their souls feel that they must gain the whole world.

That is one philosophy, one religion. What have we to oppose to the advance of this colossal mob psychology? For the first line of our defenses is not material, but spiritual.

Well, we have no regimented front to present to that spreading frenzy nor a complete national accord to oppose to it. But we do have an idea, which is more or less our national faith, though it is not exclusively our own. It is a slow and painful birth of ages of human aspiration and struggle; but, transplanted to our new soil, it grew and flourished until it became almost a religion with us and was not so long ago a beacon of hope to the rest of the world.

And what is that idea? It is the simple and revolutionary idea, or set of ideas, that man is not a means to an end, not something to be exploited by class or by state whether for wealth or for war, but an end in himself; that the highest of values on this earth is the preciousness of human life; that the only morality, the only justice, which is built upon a rock is that which respects the sacredness of the human personality; that law as an institution and states are of his own making, and exist for him, not he for them; and that the first business of men living together, the first business of the state, is not to coerce him under the despotism of the regimented mob for any ulterior purpose but to cherish and promote his individual freedom to grow in peace into the full stature of his being.

That idea, which we name democracy, has never been realized in fact. Democracy is not an accomplished thing, not an established thing. Rather it is a dynamic faith which has always had to do battle. Just now it has its back to the wall abroad, and we ourselves honor it as much in the breach as in the observance.

If we really believe in it, and God help us if we don't, then our first line of defense is to make this principle so vital a thing in our national consciousness and so effective a thing in action that its destructive opposite can find no soil of faithlessness or disaffection in which to root itself. To say that democracy does not work, and that there isn't anything that we can do about it, is simply to say that we are too indifferent, too irresolute, too spiritless to do anything about it. What democracy always needs and what it needs desperately now is a fighting heart. Remember that it is out of the soil of mental and moral disintegration, apathy, and defeatism that the noxious weed of despotism has sprung and spread.

What then is our second line of defense? It is to implement our national faith with adequate armaments, so that we will be in a position to say in language that will be heard, that any treaty, such as the Pact of Paris, entered into under the authority of the United States, is the supreme law of our land and that behind it is not only our national honor but our national power.

It is tragic to have to say that it is no time for a peace-seeking nation to disarm when the Nazi government tells the German people that they must prefer bullets to butter, when the nations that are hell-bent for war are throwing half and more than half their national resources into the building of engines of destruction. We must be in a strong position to aid in the quarantine of an international plague and in the prevention of its further spread.

Not that anyone in his senses thinks of carrying war into Germany or Italy or Japan. Nor can anyone in his senses imagine that the United States or England or France can accomplish this quarantine by each going it alone in an armament race. That is clearly the way of universal destruction.

But who dares say that it could not be done if these great powers, together with the smaller nations which stand for peace, could say with one mighty voice to the gangster nations, "So far you shall go and no further"?

Even the joint withholding of the raw materials of war

from criminal aggressors would be sufficient to check their advance, to say nothing of backing up such a measure by collective force.

I am one of those who feel that the league for world peace, the League of Nations, now lies dead or sleeping because of our absence from it. In every crisis, it has been weak because of our absence from it. In every crisis, it has been weak because it lacked our strength. Even at this moment, it could be reviewed and made an overwhelming force with our support.

But if this be an empty dream, there is still the possibility of cooperation with other like-minded nations through what Secretary Hull calls parallel action on our part. Such cooperation is, however, impossible under our so-called Neutrality Act. But there is an increasing dissatisfaction with the working of that act, an awakening to the fact that it operates in favor of strong aggressors and against weaker peoples who want only to be left alone. The first step necessary to international concert of action is the repeal of our neutrality law.

But, it is objected, if we do not rely upon ourselves alone, whom can we rely upon? France is panicky and unstable. But would France be panicky and unstable if France did not stand alone? We are told that the British government has been shifty and spineless. Shifty and spineless it has been, but would it have been if the English could have felt that they stood shoulder to shoulder with the United States? Did they not feel impelled to make terms with Fascist powers because they had lost all hope of coming to terms of cooperation with us? When shall we stop this scapegoat business, and begin searching our own hearts?

But our peace-at-any-price isolationists tell us that we must remain aloof from any measure which might give the least offense to war-loving and war-propagating governments lest we risk being involved in war. Good God, is there no risk to us in crawling into our own dugout while civilization crashes about our ears?

There is, as far as I can see, but one hope for world peace and for our own peace, and that is to join to the other like-minded peoples the moral force and the potential power of the strongest nation on this planet today.

NATIONALISM AND EDUCATION

We may be able some time really to think in terms of the world as one great neighborhood. At the moment this is but a dream for the future. Whether we like it or not, nationalism is rampant everywhere. And clearly our first duty as Americans is to set our own house in order.

For this is not sufficient to set up a new code. We must by sustained and reasonable effort develop out of ourselves a national espirit de corps—a feeling, a consciousness, that our country is a partnership of all its citizens in quest of the good life. Here lies the great opportunity and the great responsibility especially of our schools, colleges, and universities.

I do not mean that we should emulate that nationalism, now so dangerous to the peace and happiness of mankind, which in effect promotes national unity and loyalty through prejudice and hatred or contempt of other peoples and races. I mean rather that nationalism which makes every one of us share in the spirit of our country to the extent of working to cherish and preserve and promote it as one of the most precious things in the world. That there is in the American story a soul or spirit which can breathe into us sound love of country and proud devotion to its mission, I fully and reverently believe.

·IV·

NORLIN'S PHILOSOPHY

MAN'S PLACE IN NATURE

Throughout the history of the medieval church and of the medieval age there was little or no thought of progress in our sense of the word, no thought of gradual improvement of our life on the earth, no concern save to deliver mankind from "the world, the flesh and the devil" into the life to come. Earthly existence was disparaged as in itself mean and worthless, and hope built its castles beyond the grave.

The renaissance marked a reaction toward a saner view of the power of man's intellect and of the value and dignity of life on this earth, and so prepared the way for our modern habit of thinking. But the idea of progress as it is popularly held today is hardly older than some who are now living. It is a birth of the great advancement of science and of engineering in recent times, of the use of coal and iron and steam and electricity, of the so-called industrial revolution which during the single century which has passed since the day of Napoleon, and largely during our own generation, has wrought an infinitely greater change in the circumstances and conditions of human life than is to be found in the thousands of years of recorded history before Napoleon's time.

Of all the changes which this revolution has caused, the most radical change is in our conception of man's place in nature. Our conquest of nature—our rapid subjection of the very elements to our use and to our will—has delivered man from his oppressive sense of slavery to the blind forces of a hostile world and enthroned him, in his own imagination, upon the footstool of the Almighty.

But of all times this is no time for us to take things

Norlin (left) building the fireplace for his cabin at the faculty ranch

lying down. If Mr. Wells is right in saying that history is a race between education and catastrophe—and I believe that this voices a sober optimism—then this great hope is a fair challenge to the soldier which is in every one of us seeking a cause worthy of his courage. There is no cosmic law impelling us, no matter what we do, towards the ideal any more than there is a cosmic law driving us, in spite of ourselves, downward to destruction. Evolution, as far as humanity is concerned, is in our hands to direct and determine. The kingdom of heaven is not outside of us but within us, and whether we help to bring it to pass depends upon what you and I, God helping us, think and say and do. And, mind you, there is in our nature something which is quite as real as any cosmic force, something which I like to think of as God in us, an instinct for perfection, a discontent with things as they are, a desire to leave the world better than we find it, which we may safely take to be our guide—our pillar of fire by night and our pillar of cloud by day.

MAN AS CREATOR OF A BETTER LIFE

The question is, of course, whether human life is but an accident, and perhaps an unwelcome accident, in the universe, "an itch upon a single nothing"; or, rather, the question is, and this is the great question, whether we are willing to have it so.

Certainly there is no proof or hint of proof that our willingness to have it so, even if such a spirit of defeatism should result in the extinction of our human kind, would disturb the serenity of the universe. The sun and the stars and the planets would sweep proudly through space as they now do, indifferent to the fact that there would be none to behold and measure their comings and goings, or to marvel at the glory of the heavens. The earth itself would continue placidly in its orbit with no sense of bereavement.

The universe, as we know it from science, does not care in the least about us. Its framework is aflame with millions of blazing fires which are intolerant of life. So far as we can tell, only one little speck in all this vast immensity permits the existence of living organisms. The earth harbors all manners of life, but the earth shows no partiality to human life. The providence which modern science discovers in nature seems not more provident of man than of the centipede or the boll weevil or the tubercle bacillus. The late dean of St. Paul's has reminded us that "a microbe had the honor of killing Alexander the Great at the age of thirty-three, and so changing the whole course of history," and that the microbes are busy still. Indeed, there is a not unlikely prospect that the insects and parasites, having no scruples of meekness or pacifism, will inherit the earth unless we, the human kind, can make a brave fight of it together instead of turning our weapons upon ourselves, as we now do.

What is meant by our living according to nature? Does it mean that we should live according to our human nature, which some have called divine, or does it mean that we should align ourselves with the parasitic and brutish forces of which fascism itself is a manifestation?

"In harmony with Nature?" Restless fool,
Who with such heat dost preach what were to thee,
When true, the last impossibility—
To be like Nature strong, like Nature cool!

Know, man hath all which Nature hath, but more,
And in the more lie all his hopes of good.
Nature is cruel, man is sick of blood;

. . . .

Man must begin, know this, where Nature ends;
Nature and Man can never be fast friends.
Fool, if thou canst not pass her, rest her slave.

Man is of nature, and also above nature. The efforts of man, in his thinking, to explain himself in terms of the brute creation have never been convincing; and the efforts of man, in his doing, to find his satisfactions in sheer animality have always ended with dust and ashes in the mouth. Some things he has in common with all living things. On the lower plane of his being he is predacious and brutal. In such respects he is like any snake in the grass. Indeed, it might be said that in the wilderness of the impulses which pull him this way and that, he is not unlike those freakish snakes which nature now and then allows to be born—snakes with more heads than one, each head fighting the other for the food which goes into a common belly.

But man is infinitely more than that, and "in that more lie all his hopes of good." "What a piece of work is a man! how noble in reason! how infinite in faculty! in form and moving how express and admirable! in action how like an angel! in apprehension how like a god!"—man as artist, mind you, not a man who is recreant to his human self, not a biped who has reverted to, or never emerged from, brutishness and barbarism, but man as the creator of a freer and better life for man.

Man in that sense—that is to say, man not only as creature but as creator—may be truly son of God, as religion teaches. But whatever view we take of him, he is the finest thing we know in the heavens above or in the earth beneath. Let not the immensity of his soul shrink before the immensity of the universe which his own brain; ranging beyond the flaming battlements of space,

The raconteur

has measured and mapped out. He is greater than the sun, which once he worshipped, greater than all the wild forces which he once sought to appease by human sacrifice, greater than fire and flood, than famine and pestilence, and greater even than the powers of death which are devised and unloosed by the diabolisms of men.

DEMOCRACY: A DYNAMIC FAITH

For democracy is more a vision than a fact—the unquenchable vision of a society which exists to hold in leash our baser selves and give wings (to use Lincoln's phrase) to the better angels of our nature.

I can imagine that when you read these words, you will say to yourself with the smiling allowance for my years, "the old pater, bless him, is dreaming again in a world that is gone. Wings? Only the vultures have wings. The so-called democracies wriggle and cringe in their irresolution and seeking to hide away from danger. There is no united front anywhere. Even in our own country there is no vision to unite us; there is only a deafening cacophony of quarreling voices." Is this confusion, you are asking yourself, democracy? Is this the thing that I am coerced into giving my best years to, perhaps my life? If this is democracy it does not, to say the least, strike fire.

Yes, I agree. But it was not very long ago when we read together with mutual delight John Buchan's *Pilgrim's Way*. Don't you remember his saying that democracy is not in itself the good life but that it offers the best way to the good life? Unhappily most of us are prone to think that democracy is what we have, the status quo. But in a true democracy there is no status quo. Democracy is not a static thing; it is not an established thing. It is a dynamic faith, a militant faith which has ever battled and will continue to battle, never quite victorious but never driven from the field, against all the sinister forces, whether exercised in peace or in war and whether threatening from within or from without our borders, that in effect put chains upon us and prevent us from growing into the full stature of our being. It is not an end. The "American Way of Life," which we talk about so glibly, is not a stopping place. It is a road to march on, not to Utopia, but towards making more tolerable the struggle of our mankind upon this painful earth. To keep that road open and so give scope to our hopes and aspirations is, in my thinking, the never-ending quest, the great adventure—our overwhelming cause. . . .

· V ·

CHARGE TO THE GRADUATES

It has become a tradition to conclude the commencement ceremonies at the University of Colorado by reading Norlin's Charge to the Graduates. *Norlin gave this for the first time in 1935 as the conclusion of a baccalaureate address. Later, President Robert L. Stearns revised it slightly to make it more suitable for a commencement ceremony. The original follows.*

Receiving a gift from Charles Beise, President of the student body, University of Colorado, to celebrate Norlin's return to duty after a long illness (circa 1931)

But you—you are not tired. You have youth: you have strength: you have zest, courage, I trust. You go into an insecure world. Yes, but what a world to fight in and fight for! And you go not alone. The university goes with you. You take the university with you.

It is all wrong to think of commencement as the beginning of your life apart from the university, as if you were leaving the university behind. The world has no meaning historically, and should not have in our thoughts. Rather, tomorrow, the day of your commencement, is the day of your initiation in the fullest sense into the fellowship of the university. Wherever you go, there goes the university. Wherever you are, there is the university at work. Let that thought be with you always.

SOURCES

The Proper Role of College Athletics. An address to the University of Colorado students, January 8, 1929. *University of Colorado Bulletin*, Vol. 29, No. 2 (1928).

The Purpose of a University. An assembly address, 1930. *University of Colorado Bulletin*, Vol. 31, No. 2 (1931).

The Role of a State University. An unpublished speech (*circa* 1939–1940). University of Colorado, Norlin Library, Western Historical Collections, Norlin archives.

The Value of Traditional Subjects. An address to the Colorado Teachers' Association, November 1911. *Higher and Professional Education.*

Liberal Scholars as Teachers. *School and Society*, Vol. 25 (January 22, 1927), pp. 1–5.

The Value of the Classics. *Things in the Saddle* (Cambridge: Harvard University Press, 1940), pp. 43–46.

Whom, Then, Do I Call Educated? *Integrity in Education* (New York: Macmillan, 1926), pp. 5–6.

Thoughts of One in Solitary Confinement. An unpublished manuscript. Norlin archives, Box 3. University of Colorado, Norlin Library, Western Historical Collections.

Our National Defenses. *International Conciliation*, No. 341 (June 1, 1938).

Nationalism in Education. Commencement address, August 29, 1933.

Man's Place in Nature. *A Fighting Faith*, Rice Institute (July 1938), pp. 135–37.

MAN AS CREATOR OF A BETTER LIFE. An unpublished manuscript. Norlin archives, Box 3. University of Colorado, Norlin Library, Western Historical Collections.

DEMOCRACY: A DYNAMIC FAITH. University of Colorado, Norlin Library, Western Historical Collections, Norlin archive. An unpublished letter to an imaginary son (*circa* 1941–1942). Probably the last thing Norlin wrote.

CHARGE TO THE GRADUATES. Baccalaureate address, June 1935. Printed as a pamphlet. Undated. No imprint. Norlin archives. University of Colorado, Norlin Library, Western Historical Collections.